EXPAT

LIFE

Expat Life:

At Home in

San Miguel de Allende

by

John Scherber

San Miguel Allende Books
San Miguel de Allende
Guanajuato, Mexico

ACKNOWLEDGMENTS

Any book starts as an idea, and by its completion becomes a joint effort.

Thanks to my wife, Kristine Scherber, for her editorial and critical help and for the interior design of the print edition of this book.
Cover Design by Lander Rodriguez
Web Page Design by Julio Mendez

Thanks to Daniel Rueffert for the use of his cover painting titled *Las Monjas* that is so complimentary to my more literary view.
Thanks to Charles Thomas for connecting me to some of the expats.
Thanks to my readers, who have asked repeatedly over the years, when is the sequel coming?

And most of all, thank you to all those expats who shared their stories with me

ISBN: 978-0-9906551-8-3

WEBSITE

www.sanmiguelallendebooks.com

Also by John Scherber

FICTION

(The Paul Zacher Murder in México mystery series)

Twenty Centavos

The Fifth Codex

Brushwork

Daddy's Girl

Strike Zone

Vanishing Act

Jack and Jill

Identity Crisis

The Theft of the Virgin

The Book Doctor

The Predator

The Girl from Veracruz

Angel Face

Uneasy Rider

Lost in Chiapas

The Jericho Journals

Noble Rot

Twilight at Tikal

Death in the Third Act
Scorpion Rising
The Dead Pool
The Missing Matisse

The Devil's Workshop
Eden Lost
The Amarna Heresy
Beyond Terrorism: Survival

(The Townshend Vampire Trilogy)
And Dark My Desire
And Darker My Wrath

NONFICTION

San Miguel de Allende: A Place in the Heart
*A Writer's Notebook: Everything I Wish Someone
Had Told Me When I Was Starting Out*
*Into the Heart of Mexico: Expatriates Find
Themselves off the Beaten Path*
Living in San Miguel: The Heart of the Matter

Table of Contents

INTRODUCTION

As American expatriates living full time in México, my wife and I moved to San Miguel de Allende in the summer of 2007, defying both the warnings of the popular media and the conventional U.S. government "wisdom" about living south of this complex and misunderstood line we call the border. From this more southerly side, officially it's called *la frontera*, but more colloquially, *la linea*, the line.

While many will wish to see it as no more than an irregular track on a map, traveling from the Gulf to the Pacific, the truth is that the border is a line densely burdened not only with the weight of history, as we shall see, but with varying meanings for different people today. For some it is the beginning of a dream, whether they are crossing going north or going south. It can also be a foggy lens through which we view each other with fluctuating degrees of distortion and illusion, and too often with little understanding or sympathy. It is a tangible line on which we can hang our prejudices and misconceptions as if they were old suits of clothes we can never quite bring ourselves to dispose of. And it can still sometimes be, as it has too often been in the past, a provocative line drawn in the sand. That feature seems to be developing more today as I write this.

A less common way of looking at it is one I want to examine in some detail in this book. It is the idea of México as the home for expatriates, mainly Americans, but to Canadians and others as well, who wish to begin or have already begun a new life away from the country of their birth, and discovered this quite foreign place as their home. How does that work, and why is it the case? Even having gone through it myself, I can see how it still seems like a daunting prospect for some people.

I am a storyteller both by my inclination and my trade, and this is a book that examines some aspects of the expatriate experience I haven't dealt with in my three other books about living in México. It is not intended to be a sequel, but more as a companion piece that can be profitably read even by those who have read the others, since there is little or no overlap, other than in my own attitudes and insights, which continue to evolve year by year, and book by book.

As the author of thirty-three other books, the process of writing is always important to me. I don't start the first paragraph or even the first sentence without knowing who would want to read this. It is written for people who are curious about why a rational person (like me) would leave the country he grew up in, one he inhabited all of his life in order to live in strange settings among people who neither share many of his values, nor understand the focus of his lifestyle, nor his need to explain what goes on to those neighbors from the north who might also wish to visit or live here. To leave a country in which he operated three entrepreneurial businesses, raised a family, wrote several books, and was an active participant in what we then called The American Dream. It is the story of the kind of experiences that await that incautious type of person who settles on this side (my side) of that porous fence we call the border.

It is a book written for anyone considering such a chancy move—but just how risky is it? What kind of person does well as an expatriate and even prospers during that awkward phase of transition, and afterward? How do such people come to earth and get involved? Being an immigrant may be much like going through puberty. You know your voice will change, since Spanish requires a different kind of timbre and inflection, but what other physical and mental transformations await the unwary expat? Why would any reasonable person consider going through that, especially later in life? And has politics now assumed a higher position among the list of reasons why people decide to leave the United States? It was thinking about that possibility that prompted me to revisit the subject in the light of today, as it occurred to me that "home" as we once thought of it may be less homelike for many than it once was. What if home as we knew it has evolved away from us, even as we still search for what it once meant? This is a question I cannot answer for all of us, but in this volume other expats will speak to that issue.

When my wife and I left Minnesota for San Miguel de Allende in the state of Guanajuato in 2007 it was not for political reasons. We had vacationed in México a dozen times over as many years before we decided to relocate there once the kids were established on their own. We sold our house easily without realizing that the residential real estate market was near the top of its arc in that particular cycle, and we left town with no great sense of stress or transition. We were abundantly ready for a change, but to us that mainly meant we planned to settle into the culture and climate of our southern neighbor with no regrets. We knew it would not be easy, but our history of repeated visits had made us think we could take a shot at it without beginning as complete newbies. I don't recall that we were at all fearful of making the move. Nothing we have learned since has contradicted that, even though being here has often contradicted our expectations.

While neither of us was enthusiastic about the tone of party politics as then practiced in the United States on either side, the George W. Bush presidency had left us confused and disengaged. While I had been, over the course of my life, both a Democrat and a

Republican, I could never understand what Bush stood for. I felt early on that the invasion of Iraq was a false flag venture that further destabilized a tensely unbalanced region, and the removal of the iron-fisted dictator Saddam Hussein exposed the population to even greater miseries and uncertainties. We still live with that legacy today and the entire area offers no sign of opting for peace. Nor do the great powers seem inclined to halt their meddling.

Living in México has offered us a means of paying less attention to these problems without actually gaining any further distance from them. We're now only slightly more removed from those intractable conflicts in a world that's growing smaller all the time. It is quite possible that there is nowhere left to hide, but that may be the subject of a different book, possibly one of my twenty-some mysteries.

In the intervening years in the United States we have seen an explosion of the national debt and an ongoing reduction of the middle class. As an American couple living in voluntary exile in a Mexican town with a substantial expatriate community, it seems that we're observing the gradual decline of a system in the States that is losing its ability to be inclusive, or even to *appear* inclusive, no matter which party is in power. I'm sure there is a message in that, but I leave it to others to spell out what it might be. The certain and continuing deterioration of civility in politics has left me looking for more rewarding subjects to explore. It is in that spirit that I'm happy to return to considering the nuances of expat life in México.

It is not the point of this book to probe the reasons for the election of Donald Trump, or to analyze the effect of his policies, with a single exception: that since the defeat of the Democrats in both the White House and in Congress, there has developed a noticeably greater interest in moving to México among Americans. Is that only chatter? I'm not going to speculate about that in this introduction. I'm sure that as we proceed people will tell me why they have come here, or wish to come here. This is in spite of the unrelenting attacks on México by the U.S. press and the State Department, and now by the President himself. As we will see in more detail, this antagonism is nothing new, and it should not be a cause for surprise to anyone who knows a little of the history of this hemisphere. (See Chapter Two)

The question that is forming in my mind is whether a different version of the American expat is coming here now, one with different aims and hopes than my wife and I had in 2007. Is there a sea change of some kind underway because of political developments in the United States? Is the real character of that country moving further away from the manner in which we've always thought of it, or wished to think of it? Or is it only the government that is moving away, while the people, the bedrock of American society, watch with a confused and increasingly concerned expression? Is it therefore now easier to think that a country as foreign as México could be home?

Many people both in and out of the media have remarked that democracy is dead in the United States, not just stylishly radical thinkers or people of a pessimistic turn of mind. Recently I heard former President Carter say this. But México, with its long history of revolution and unstable government, is not a logical choice for those seeking a system of governance unfailingly true to its founding principles. Perhaps no country is. Those of us who have immigrated here love México for other reasons, just as there are still many reasons to love the U.S. beyond its current toxic political climate.

Some of the questions I will try to address in this book are: Who are the new expatriates? Are they merely the current generation of the old ones, using different hairstyles, tattoos, and buzzwords? What changes in their lives do they expect to find here as the result of their move? Will those changes be caused by their position in this culture or their need for flight? To what degree are politics in the U.S. a motive for their presence? What aspects of Mexican culture and society are not likely to be obvious to them, but will ultimately need their serious attention? And ultimately, where and what is home? Is it a place that we can pack up and take with us, as portable as a state of mind perhaps? Or is it something new awaiting us on the ground upon our arrival, lacking only our recognition and embrace to make it real? Isn't this an identity question? Like, who have we been in the past and who are we now? And even more, what will we become as we make this transition?

In an online dictionary I found this definition of home as the second of three, and I liked it best: *the place in which one's domestic affections are centered.* That in itself suggests that home is something to be found rather than something to bring along in a cart or a semi trailer. It's not part of our luggage. I like that idea because it rests on a less inward view, and I would hope that coming to live in México would draw us out of ourselves more than it drives us back within. We want to be open to the experience, cautious perhaps, without being guarded, a task not so easy later in life, but still a useful one at any time.

In the style of my other books about expat life in México, this is not intended to be in any way a scientific sample. I have no background in statistics, and whatever conclusions I come to will be the product of my own experience on the scene here over more than eleven years, my powers of observation as the author of thirty-three other books, and my personal commitment to tell the truth as well as I am able to discern it. I operate with no political party bias. While I am always alert to issues and personalities, I try hard not to label people. I also resent being labeled by them, although many have tried with little success. Labels are our most common means of dismissal. They are a form of blinders for the labeler, a kind of self-censorship.

As in my fiction, I have little interest in thinking collectively or generalizing. Discovering the truth always works best in the details, with the specific person, the individual. We learn most easily about other people and ourselves from our face-to-face contacts.

For several years I have endeavored to stand outside the circle of American politics because I find it toxic and uncivil on both sides. The two major parties have adopted as their chief objective the thorough division of Americans into irreconcilable camps where sane conversation across the gulf that separates them is no longer possible. I believe this has been done with intent. If we cannot listen to other views, we will not know what is going on, and we will have no other views to compare ours with. That encourages the growth of unchallenged folly.

In contrast, my position is that I am willing to talk civilly with anyone who can be civil to me. The conversational parts of this book that follow are framed in that spirit.

There are approximately one million Americans living legally in México, and many others who are not here legally. For there is not only the much more publicized issue of unofficially admitted Mexicans living under the radar in the U.S., there is also the fact that it is even easier to live illegally here in México, although harder to vote. The bureaucracy is often inefficient and its Achilles heel is that government agencies do not easily share information with each other.

Where I have conversations in this book, they are with people living in the San Miguel area. To some degree they are representative of Americans anywhere in México, but not consistently and never entirely so. It will be easy to find expatriates in many other places who do not think like their peers do here, and this book may speak for them only partially or not at all. An entire subset of expatriates lives in parts of México that offer little or no support from other expats. They usually try hard to leave no footprint on the culture. (See my book, *Into the Heart of México: Expatriates Find Themselves off the Beaten Path*).

Call this excursion then a sampler of the motives, hopes, and experiences of expats living in San Miguel, whether recently arrived or not. It examines the lifestyle of a selected few. My selection process has aimed for diversity and comparison, but it will not equip the reader to make broad generalizations of what brought and what keeps people here. As a writer primarily of fiction, I'm not fond of broad statements, and for me they carry little weight. As I suggested above, my approach is always that of the novelist, where the truth is revealed more vividly in the detail of the story rather than in the generalizations latent in the stroke of a broader brush.

Before we consider in detail where we are today, let's start with a few thoughts about where we've been.

PART ONE

PLACES

CHAPTER ONE
WHERE HAVE WE BEEN?

For nearly three hundred years, from the early 1600s until the late 1890s, Americans were headed west. Without knowing much about it, people were mostly agreed that the future lay there. The political, military, and cultural forces all seemed to be aligned to promote that impulse. The phrase, "wide open spaces," was originated then, and it was a relatively new concept, certainly one that had never been heard in the densely populated quarters of old Europe.

During the nineteenth century millions of immigrants entered on the East Coast, caught their breath, perhaps put down roots for a while as they rebuilt their finances and learned English, and then they or their children often assembled a grubstake and left in search of the frontier. The frontier was the place at the edge of things, where law and order ran out, and where they were more on their own than they were probably ready for, even if in those early years they were only a hundred miles inland from the Atlantic shore.

The common impulse was for people to put more

space between each other. Europe had long been crowded and land availability had always been controlled by the gentry. Since agriculture was still the basis of most large fortunes, land was therefore hard to get if you were not in line to inherit any.

In Minnesota, where I grew up, two of our much-revered pioneer statesmen made their fortunes by buying up Indian land at auction from the U.S. government. After the disastrous (for both sides) Sioux War of 1862, the indigenous people were pushed back further and the land they had held under treaty was confiscated and sold to both individual pioneers and to speculators. Our two statesmen bought a great deal of it, usually for twelve and a half cents an acre, and advertised it in Europe for one dollar an acre. Even at eight times their cost, it was correctly perceived as an extraordinary bargain abroad, although it offered no physical improvements whatever: no roads, bridges, or wells. It still presented a compelling inducement to emigrate for people who had never had the slightest hope of getting any land for themselves. I can imagine that few of them were at all realistic about the trials awaiting them on arrival. More than anything else, it all looked like hope.

Yet, even with this naively expansionist outlook, the melting pot was still a viable and rational goal, if in practice if took a couple of generations to achieve. Immigrant Americans wanted to be connected with their new culture and nation, even if they couldn't quite imagine the blended result.

Although it had at one time seemed nearly endless, about 125 years ago the frontier ran out. Our task since then has been to learn how to arrange ourselves in a compatible and functional fashion upon that new American terrain. Depending on where you look, it has worked with varying degrees of success.

For several generations, as the young United States sought to navigate unmolested through a world dominated by European power politics, the answer to the question of where we were going appeared to be that we were going "our own way." If not everyone would've defined that way in the same manner, that didn't matter. We all by our nature had an idea of what that meant. Even if something of a blend, there was still a discernible "American Way" evolving. Framed against a waving stars and stripes, you could even see it later in the slogans surrounding Superman in his comic books, where it was accompanied, as if assembled into a new divine trinity, by its coequal partners in virtue; Truth, Justice, and the American Way. This was the beginning of American exceptionalism. We were not just like everyone else.

Initially for America to operate on such a platform it seemed that isolationism was required to avoid social and cultural contamination from older (and possibly exhausted, both intellectually and morally) nations.

We did not care to be part of history any longer, thank you very much. Quite visibly, it had never worked that well anyway, and the Europeans still appeared to carry around far too much of it for their own good. As someone once remarked about the Balkans, "They generate more history than they can consume."

But in the midst of two mainly European conflagrations, WWI and WWII (or perhaps that was only one with a breather, a time to bury the dead and reload?) we elected two presidents who both quietly understood that isolation was an impossible policy if we were to nurture any vestige of our own founding principles on European soil. They were Woodrow Wilson and Franklin Roosevelt.

Sadly, as it soon became clear, being caught up in other people's history was inevitable after all, whether we liked it or not. But that left Americans in a position where they had to define themselves in ways that went beyond merely saying what we were not; for example, that we were neither Nazis nor Communists.

So what are we? The governmental system set up by our Constitution provides a bilateral focus. Unlike Europe with its (apparently) devastating flaws, our founders avoided the parliamentary system. Perhaps they had observed it too closely in action. After all, some of them had been born in England, and if they weren't, many had been born in British colonies including our own, where the same rules mostly applied at arm's length. Yet that imperfect parliamentary system easily provided for a multiplicity of parties, even from the point of their emergence from nothing. Every position could have a forum, a voice. In order to rule, the prime minister needed to have the support of a majority of votes in parliament commanded by those differing parties. Once he or she lost that support, a vote of no confidence would call a new election. It appeared there was genuine merit in a coalition form of government, since it was clearly more inclusive, a feature we had lost some time ago in the United States.

I can't speculate on why our founders avoided this path, but I have no reason to distrust their sincerity. They were faced with an enormous pioneering job in a threatening time, and they very well knew it. From their writings we can see that few of them shrank from moral or ethical complexity. They passed the slavery issue down the road because they knew it could not be solved then and to attempt it guaranteed a fatal barrier to unity among the colonies in a time of war with England. Even though the failure to end slavery was a tragedy for its victims, that delay was also an act of realism, not one of cowardice.

Still, as it developed, what they gave us instead is a system that favors two large dominant parties, although that may have meant little to the founders at the time. Yes, we can have as many other parties as we wish, but they have trouble being heard. In the most recent presidential election they were excluded from the debates, for no good reason that I can see, other than that they were bound to raise issues inconvenient to the others. These would've included matters of deep concern to a large segment of the American population. The further development of small or emerging parties is hampered because they cannot receive matching campaign funds from the Federal Government if they don't achieve a five percent vote in the primaries. The cards are stacked against them, much like piles of greenbacks.

While the parliamentary system requires parties and individuals of diverse views to work together to achieve power, our system now runs (I won't say thrives) more and more on division. Compromise has become an obscene word, one that somehow is construed to mean betraying sacred principles. As Noam Chomsky has observed, we have now become tribal in our politics. Issues no longer matter. If our candidate is a militant Nazi child molester we will attack you viciously because your candidate is also a militant Nazi child molester. And if neither of them really is one, they will still be accused of that once the issue comes up.

It is now a time when division is no longer mainly an element of mathematics; it is a fundamental part of how things work (or don't work) in the USA. This condition does nothing to make life easier or make government, which after all is our employee, more functional. It frames our view of each other and pervades our decisions as we constantly focus on party, race, and gender as ways of labeling each other as different from us. We are slicing ourselves into thinner and thinner layers and the spaces between each one are constantly growing. The two major parties are the cheerleaders for this process as communication between and among these divisions becomes harder and harder. Sooner or later we are going to have to learn to work together again simply to get anything at all done.

I'm going to suggest that this increasingly nasty under layer of American society is one of several factors that are increasingly driving Americans to live elsewhere. There is a growing perception among people who are not committed party zealots, people who are simply looking for a satisfying way to live under an efficient government, that society does not need to be so hostile, and in fact, that it is hostility itself that is often tying us in knots. As I look back across the border, this looks less and less like what I always thought of as home.

Is it possible that the Americans who move to México are seeking to escape from history again, just as their distant forebears attempted? The history that has brought us into the grip of an aging republic whose grasp of the principles of its founders is now grown flaccid and approximate?

Part of my message in this book is this: Let's lighten up. Maybe it's time to move away from this unnecessary punch fest, one that truly does not serve any of our interests. For myself, I would not be a member of any organization that urged me to hate people that do not think the way I do. That's the bottom line.

Militants will say I'm too easy going, even dangerously naive. The enemy is out there and we damn well need to be ready to take him on the instant he makes the slightest move against us. Let's oil our guns.

Perhaps. That's also the argument that sells us the wars we have rarely needed. Did we really need to go to Vietnam? I won't revive all of that debate, but the resulting conflict at home was a societal game changer that shaped much of what we are today. What did we ever hope to achieve in Afghanistan, which is now our longest-running conflict?

CHAPTER TWO
WHERE IS HOME?

The introduction to this book raises a preliminary question for any expat: Where is home? I know it's out there somewhere, but once I've left where it used to be, how will I recognize it when I see it again, if I do?

Not long ago, here in San Miguel I attended a talk by Richard Blanco, the poet who read at President Obama's second inaugural, and again for the reopening of the U.S. Embassy in Havana. As the openly gay son of Cuban parents, born in Spain and raised in Miami, he has sufficient reason to be asking this question too, perhaps more than most of us. It is no surprise that he feels a relaxed and supportive welcome in this town of San Miguel that shelters eight or ten thousand expats, also severed to some degree from their origins, even if more as a matter of choice than when he was. What reminded me of his talk was that his family was exiled by a radical change in politics in Havana, not a slow process of decay as I described above, but rather a precipitous and violent collapse.

Blanco has resolved his search for home in a series of brilliant poems and in a book on his childhood in South Beach, a district of Miami. While his answers are uniquely his own, his questions will stimulate another series from expats already here and those in transit. Let me offer a few answers generated from my own experience:

Home may be where the heart is, but it's also where the snow isn't. I'm writing this in the middle of September, a time, when back in Minnesota, we used to be busy raking leaves. The maple trees were lovely in their red and gold hues, even as the inexorable procession of seasons filled us with dread. Because we knew exactly what was coming, we also were studiously checking the insulation in the attic. We were topping off the antifreeze in the car and making a note to use a more lightweight variety of oil at the next change. In spending fifty-eight years there I always knew I had given over too much of my life to the frigid burden of snow boots and down jackets, but in the long, demanding grip of jobs, family ties, and friendships, it was hard to find a method of release. Living in México now, I have seen how escape is accomplished by the pros when they were caught in the system—with tunnels and bribery, a means we never thought of up north. After all, the ground there was quickly frozen.

Home is where you can stop being your old self, that is, the self you thought you needed to be, the one you *had* to be to keep your career track open, to keep the neighbors from talking about you, to keep your kids in check and on the way to being good citizens of a country you were not always entirely convinced you still wanted to live in. You found yourself peddling a mantra of certainty from your own position of veiled but growing doubt, but you kept your mouth shut. You were there to give the kids a foundation of reliable values, a way to function successfully in American society, but if they wished to move on from there (as you were now quietly planning after they went to bed), that needed to be their own choice.

What we learned as we settled in was that México has a more relaxed system of identity that does not question your ability, even your absolute right to be somewhat different from the photo on your driver's license— if you've even bothered to get one here. It does not ask what you formerly did for a living. If anyone here asks you anything at all, it is what you are doing today, at this moment, at this stage of your life. Now is what matters, and no one demands to see your credentials to participate. You are, after all, alive and here even without them. You are required to prove nothing more than that.

Home is a place where you are not required to be trendy. Even if you weren't aware of needing to be trendy before, you will feel that need even less so here. Being cutting edge is only understood in reference to a machete, or to the man who makes the rounds of the neighborhoods on his bicycle, blowing a harsh whistle, ready to grind your expensive German cutlery to a fine and rapidly diminishing edge for ten pesos, which is today about fifty-two cents U.S. After around six of his visits you will be carving your pot roast with a pricy set of icepicks.

Home is where not everything works. Yes, that is true, but I wonder if it is any different here? It certainly differs in which things don't work and which do. It works, for example, to pay five dollars a month here for water that we can't drink. When we lived in a suburb of Minneapolis, Minnesota, we paid ninety-nine dollars a month for water we also couldn't drink (for different reasons—it tasted vile), but the bill for which was delivered with a nice bi-monthly color brochure that told us how great it was. Like a bad entertainer with a good agent, it came with a press release. We used to keep that shameless piece of propaganda on top of the five-gallon water bottle in our kitchen dispenser, the one we bought weekly from someone else at extra cost. At least we felt better about it. Here in México we don't feel as good when things don't work, but we do know we're getting a much better deal on failure. Even bad things are cheaper here, and that's always worth something.

Here the power goes out just long enough to require us to reset all the clocks. Everything you buy now has a clock on it that needs to be reset. There is no reason for this, except possibly to remind you that you're living at the whim of the chancy power grid of México. In Minnesota we lived in a wooded neighborhood where the power lines had naïvely been run through the trees rather than buried. Every time a high wind came through, the lines went down when dead branches fell on them. One weekend in May we had houseguests for three days and our power was out the entire time. I did a run to a boutique coffee shop every morning, cursing.

In the eighties there was a movie I never saw called Stop Making Sense, featuring The Talking Heads. The irreverent perspective of its title has stayed with me. Since the turnout didn't demand a sequel, I believe the entire film crew must've drifted down to México and infiltrated the government after shooting ended, where they remain firmly in control today. Their fine management style can also be observed in all the utility companies. More of that later.

These are superficial signs of home. Richard Blanco was talking more deeply about identity and how it plugs into our sense of place and family. In our second decade as willing exiles we think of home as a portable unit, self-contained, and in this country, run by solar energy. We love the sun. We need the sun, because central heating rarely penetrates this far south.

Home is a shell that protects us from inclement

weather, but more importantly, it harbors our ambitions, supports our dreams, and nurses our hopes as creative people living atypical lives among kindly strangers who know we have money to spend. It travels well, because as compact as it is, home still provides sufficient room for all of our essentials, even if we would prefer to buy our jeans in Laredo.

At the heart of this durable shell is our personal identity, which is the essence of home. It is not the title we have, or what we own, or the image we wish to project; but what we do every day of our lives. That defines us as the individuals we are. And we are all individuals before we are Americans, Canadians, women or men, adults or children, Catholics or Moslems, Democrats or Republicans.

Home is where we choose to live today, not what we left behind. The people who will do best in México are the ones who discover that much sooner than others.

CHAPTER THREE
THE BORDER IN MOTION

H aving glanced at the present, and at a question that is fundamental to all of us, let's continue by glancing back at who we were and where we came from, because we bring this history like unwanted baggage into México when we arrive; it is a part of our inbred attitude that we may not be aware of, even though we may have heard parts of it all our lives. The complete story appears to be more than the sum of its parts.

For the young United States, the entire nineteenth century was a period of explosive territorial growth. George Washington, a land surveyor by his original trade, had always believed that our future lay in the west. The trend was officially launched with considerable foresight by Thomas Jefferson in the Louisiana Purchase of 1803. He was shrewd enough to recognize that Napoleon needed money to finance his ongoing European wars. The Louisiana Territory, which the French emperor had forced the Spanish to return just three years earlier (it had been a concession from France after the

Seven Years War ending in 1763), provided a way to raise funds with little threat to fundamental French ambitions. Napoleon's determination to reframe the map of Europe had focused his attention more on continental issues than on the colonial world overseas. Bear in mind that France had recently lost Haiti to a murderous slave revolt that had begun in 1791 (during the heart of the French revolution), and so their latest colonial challenge had been a scene of utter and shocking disaster. After the earlier loss of their Canadian holdings to England, they may understandably have felt that having their main field of operations closer to home might be more productive. This was reinforced by the fact that the British navy was still master of the Atlantic during this period.

Jefferson had served as ambassador to France in the early years of American independence, from 1785-9. Although his grand territorial acquisition was unsuccessfully opposed by some in Congress on the grounds that it exceeded presidential authority, it more than doubled the original size of the thirteen colonies and advanced the process of reducing European influence in the Western Hemisphere, one of his secondary goals.

Next came the purchase of Florida from Spain, completed by President James Monroe in 1819 for $5 million. Part of the same trend was that in 1823 Monroe also wrote the Monroe Doctrine, the policy statement that forbade further European colonization or intervention in the Western Hemisphere on threat of a United States confrontation. While this was an overly optimistic position to take at the time, it held for nearly forty years until Maximilian of Austria took advantage of France's help to invade México while the United States was distracted by the Civil War early in the 1860s.

In 1836, with the aid of many Americans fighting unofficially, Texas seceded from México, and in 1845 it was absorbed into the United States as a state. Oregon and Washington came into our sphere in 1846 when an agreement with the British ended their claim. In the same year we engaged México in a thinly justified war connected to that same annexation of Texas, and in the process seized the northern half of their country as well. That territory covers what are now the states of California, Nevada, Arizona, New Mexico, Utah, and parts of Kansas, Colorado and Wyoming.

In 1853-4 we purchased for $10 million (forty-six cents an acre), a strip of land of just under 30,000 square miles forming a new boundary along the base of Arizona and half of New Mexico (the Gadsden Purchase), and so México experienced its third major loss of territory to the U.S. within the space of seventeen years.

In 1867 we purchased Alaska from the Russians for $7.2 million (two cents an acre). In 1893, a coup partly composed of U.S. businessmen overthrew the indigenous monarchy in the Hawaiian Islands, and that territory was annexed to the United States as a territory five years later. In the Spanish American War of the same year of 1898, a ten-week conflict precipitated by our intervention in a Cuban move for independence, we seized Cuba, the Philippines, Guam, and Puerto Rico from the crumbling Spanish empire.

In terms of expansion, this was a hectic ninety-five years. These acquisitions were usually justified by the phrase, *Manifest Destiny*. In this usage, *manifest* meant obvious, although it may not have been so obvious to all our neighbors that were so diminished in territory and independence as a result of these encounters.

Throughout this period, within the U.S. borders, tens of millions of acres of Indian territory, guaranteed by treaty with the federal government, were confiscated by force and resettled by whites. Andrew Jackson was a leader in this process, and he rode his resulting popularity to the White House.

It should be no surprise that their part in this experience may collectively constitute a kind of speed bump in the national consciousness of many Mexicans, to say nothing of other neighbors. If there exists a tendency south of the border to think of the U.S. as a rapacious and implacable neighbor, one best regarded with caution and at arm's length, we can understand how this view might have developed over generations.

Not so widely known is that the most recent

American invasion of México occurred in 1914, when U.S. naval forces occupied the city of Veracruz for seven months. The issue was a minor dispute involving the detention of a small number of U.S. sailors who had entered a restricted area in a different part of the country. The response from the Woodrow Wilson administration was heavy handed and arrogant, but it came at a time when our participation in World War I had not yet been launched. When the American sailors were released by the Mexican government with an apology almost immediately, the U.S. government also demanded a twenty-one-gun salute to our offshore fleet. When that was not forthcoming, the occupation followed. For once, we left México with its territory intact, even if its dignity and national pride were more than a bit disheveled.

This contentious shared history of the United States and México still shadows the difficult backdrop of the million-strong community of American expats living south of the border today. If we are still invaders, it is now on a one-by-one basis, and for once we arrive bearing a great deal of good will.

I tend to view history as a continuous fabric, where one event flows into another. While it is mainly children, politicians, and criminals who believe that actions have no consequences, to my knowledge, the law of cause and effect has never been repealed. While time does tend to mend these cross-border wounds, I can see certain attitudes still current in the United States today that retard that healing process, and thinking of my brief review above of some of the interactions between our two nations, these current attitudes have a sadly familiar look.

One way they still appear, of course, is in the stance of the U.S. media towards México. To say there is extreme bias understates the problem. It is rare to find objective press reporting on any Mexican subject, aside from sand, sun, margaritas, and palm trees in the travel magazines. The problem of Mexican drug smuggling into the United States and the American customer base it serves is blithely regarded as an exclusively Mexican problem. But isn't this like a situation where you buy a new car from the dealer and then condemn him for selling you that car? Any transaction is a two way street, and to see one side as bearing the entire responsibility for the drug trade is to wear self-serving blinders, often a feature of international relations.

The U.S. State Department plays a role in this too, with its ongoing stream of travel alerts. Certainly some of them are appropriate, but many of them are not and only serve to scare people away from México. Locals and expats alike here use a simple strategy to avoid risk that Americans also use at home. We know that every country has its trouble spots. You learn where they are and you avoid them as you go on living a perfectly normal life. Normal in terms of risk, I mean, but far above normal in terms of reward.

A few days ago I read a news article online about a Mexican issue and then scanned the comments section at the bottom. I was appalled to see line after line of the most vile and uninformed responses. All the adverse publicity from the media has certainly had some effect on people with no direct experience or knowledge of México.

Altogether we have a government and press attitude from the north of withering condescension towards México. Certainly some media figures, like Fox's former anchor, Bill O'Reilly, often engaged in nonstop rants about this country. The name itself was like a trigger that reliably set him off. From my extensive travels in México and my own long-time residence here I know that most of what he had to say on the subject was false, coming from a perspective that was at once biased and uninformed. It is a truism in marketing (and in its evil twin, propaganda) that if you repeat something often enough, people will believe it. In this case, many have.

The motives behind this barrage of negativity are not clear, although I've heard a number of plausible suggestions as to why it happens. Some have suggested that its purpose is to reduce American spending in México. I'm skeptical of this idea. If anything, I tend to see it as part of a larger ongoing American attitude that says México is a dirty, dangerous, and backward kind of place, full of lazy people; a country that could never aspire to be even second class on its best day. It sounds like it's an appropriate victim for a bully, if that's how you're inclined to act—for example, if you bill yourself as the last remaining superpower, the policeman of the world. It's the kind of arrogance and self-righteousness that is still saying, in essence, "We'll occupy one of your cities if you don't fire a twenty-one gun salute to us."

Or maybe we'll just seize another large segment of your territory. A popular bumper sticker here states, "Make America México Again."

I find it worse than embarrassing on those rare occasions when people expect that I share any of those attitudes. At the same time I never sentimentalize México. The Mexican cactus exhibits spines as well as flowers. But like other countries, it deserves to be taken on its own merits, without racist blinkers or political overtones, which are almost never honest or objective. Or in this case, even useful. We all need to take our blinkers off and look hard at the real character of our southern neighbor, because otherwise we'll never see it. Don't take anyone else's word for what this place is really like. Only experience matters.

It would be easy to say, "Well, that occupation incident in Veracruz was in 1914, more than a hundred years ago. Does it really matter anymore?" It does matter if it's part of a continuity of attitudes that changes in form over the years but not much in tone or substance.

Fortunately, many Americans choose to ignore the alarmists. In the latest full year I have data on, more than twenty million Americans visited México. While they were here they were eight times less likely to be murdered than if they had stayed home. Come down for the party, I say, and stay for the culture. And don't forget the relative safety.

Considering this difficult history, in the lengthy time of my residence here I haven't seen any signs of animosity from the Mexicans around me. I won't say it doesn't exist, but it's neither visible nor is it common.

CHAPTER FOUR
WHAT'S NOT TO LIKE ABOUT MEXICO?

Some readers tend to see me as an apologist for México, and for the San Miguel lifestyle in particular, but as with most places, it turns out that México offers a number of things that do not work very well. Like any serious writer, I am first and foremost an observer, and I have suggested several times in other places that this country ought not to be regarded as a destination for anyone searching for perfection. México does not operate that way now, and was never made that way, physically, culturally, or legally.

Like the United States and most other countries, the trappings of democracy here disguise a system of government that is operated by powerful corporate and family interests largely for their own benefit. The citizens come in a distant second. It is no coincidence that one of the richest men in the world lives in México City, and the second in Seattle. The rest of us get by on our own. Most insightful people understand that and move on with their embrace of an imperfect, if still quite rewarding, lifestyle.

Perhaps the secret is not to demand too much.

As beautiful as most of México is, there is still a serious absence of awareness of that beauty among many people. Trash is thrown freely from cars, both here in San Miguel and on the nearby highways. Driving through the open country toward the neighboring botanical gardens, for many years we saw the brush clutching at hundreds of plastic bags. While we still lived in town we picked up trash on the street in front of our house almost daily, and in one case the slippery body of a long dead goat.

The fiestas, both legendary and plentiful, provide a handy way to blow off steam for people whose jobs are often repetitive, boring, and unrewarding. May is a month where they are the most densely concentrated. I can appreciate that religious fervor provides a means of mental and spiritual escape from daily routines, and the Church and the local government have provided many opportunities. These events are colorful and entertaining, and I support their role in this culture. In fact, in our old neighborhood, we contributed every year to the flower fund for the Santa Cruz (Holy Cross) fiesta.

At the same time, they seem in my view to be too heavily dependent on rockets and fireworks of all kinds, and increasingly so. Is it possible that the largest range of religious sentiment is best expressed by explosives? Artillery barrages that begin at four AM and sometimes operate all night? Older readers of this book will appreciate it when I compare these bombardments with the Tet offensive of early 1968 in Viet Nam. I wasn't there to hear it, but the ambience must sound nearly the same. Since most of the celebrants are not well heeled, and bottle rockets are far from free, it might be good to ask who is paying for all these fireworks. Is it a way of buying votes?

Another issue is graffiti, a tiresome force in degrading the visual environment. We never had any on our house, but we often saw it nearby. Graffiti is a particularly crude way of disfiguring a neighborhood. In other places I've traveled in México, like Oaxaca, another wonderful city, it's worse. There, it more often has a political flavor. I wonder why anyone would trust the partisans of a political party to rule in the public interest when their adherents don't hesitate to vandalize the city with spray paint?

The nearby larger city of Querétaro (population, nearly one million) has done a much better job of keeping the streets clean and curbing graffiti, but the San Miguel authorities do not seem to make much effort to prevent it, although they do have an agency that is quite responsive in showing up to clean it off when called. I think it's a matter of prevention and education, more than anything else, both from the residents and the government officials. These are tiresome issues, but they are still minor matters, and a determined effort to fix them would pay off here.

Over the last few years, traffic has become a larger issue. The core of the city was laid out in the sixteenth century, and most of the streets are narrow, as fit those times. It was an era when carriages, wagons, and animals were parked within walled courtyards, not along the curb. We have a street named Mesónes in *el centro*. The word means inn. Many of the old residences there have a wide and tall entrance sill in the wall at the sidewalk. If, as you walk, you take a moment and study these thresholds you will see that that they are often cut with channels in two places to allow the passage of carriage or wagon wheels. The doors are tall enough to admit high coaches with luggage strapped on the top. The massive mesquite doors would close behind them for overnight security.

Times change. Now auto and bus traffic on these tight streets has become difficult and tiresome at times. Although some experienced and insightful people have offered several comprehensive traffic management plans, no real changes have yet been implemented. In wondering why not, it is possible to conclude that some established interests would be damaged by fixing these problems.

It is often the initial idea of people looking to move here that they want to live in the downtown district, in *el centro*. Yes, it is the most historic part, the one with the most textured nuances of old México, the one where, if you removed the vehicles and signage, it could often pass for 1700. But it is also the most crowded, the noisiest, and the most expensive. One interesting idea to consider is that none of the records set by people able to party the longest and the hardest are held by retired Americans or Canadians, anywhere.

My own concept is that when I'm finished partying I am ready to go home and go to bed, and above all else, my home will be a place where no more partying is going to happen for the rest of the night. (I'll add this to our other definitions of home.) Often if you insist on living in *el centro*, this strategy will still not get you away from the party when you're finished, so bring earplugs and a cartload of patience.

The cobblestone streets, while charmingly reminiscent of an earlier time when most vehicles were built of wood, are inexpensive to install and repair. They require no special equipment, but they are hell on motor vehicle suspensions. The money saved by the city in avoiding more serious street paving is paid back doubly by car owners over time in accelerated wear. Do not bring your restored 1956 Jaguar XK140 coupe down here, nor your Bentley Continental. Picturesque as it is, no scenes with James Bond in his vintage Aston Martin have ever been filmed in San Miguel, and for very good reason. Furthermore, choose to drive a car that can be serviced by a dealer here in town if it's still under warranty. Otherwise you will find yourself cooling your heals for an entire day in a distant and possibly charmless district of a larger town as you wait for your periodic service. The phrase to remember for routine service is "in by nine, out at six." That's nine hours waiting on a park bench.

As of this writing, the car dealers who have show-room and service facilities on San Miguel are Volkswa-gen, Chevrolet, and Nissan. That can change. When we arrived we bought a new Ford Edge here, and that dealer has now left town. For cars beyond their warranty years, there are several superb maintenance and repair garages.

Bring instead your good walking shoes, and pay careful attention to the sidewalks, where if a sudden foot-square hole should appear, placing your shoe it and breaking your ankle is legally an act of fate. It is not the fault of the person who made the sidewalk, nor of any who should have been maintaining it. This is not a cul-ture full of lawyers eager to take someone to the cleaners on your behalf for a third of the settlement. In court the judge is more likely to ask you what you were thinking when you fell into that hole, and why you had decided that being observant was not your job. Your lawyer will push your wheelchair up to the bench to respond.

More seriously, to me the worst aspect of living in México is the dense and intractable poverty in the coun-tryside. You will not see it as often in town since it costs so much, relative to local earnings, to live here (about 50% of costs in the U.S.). In the countryside, the issues are access to decent housing, clean water, and education; plus good nutrition, adequate health care, and sanitation. A substantial number of expat-based organizations work hard at combating these problems. We will examine several of them later in this book when we talk to some people who are active in their programs.

México is not a poor nation, but much too large a segment of the population is desperately so. As I have said elsewhere, there are a lot of people here with a great deal of money, and a growing middle class, but the bottom tier is still firmly at the bottom, and I don't see much upward movement there. Part of this is the class structure, which dictates that you will stay in the slot you were born in even when your finances improve, if they ever do. This condition will not easily change, so the issue is more about having a better life within the stratum of your birth. Don't think about moving on up to the east side.

Classroom attendance is compulsory through middle school but not after, and it is no longer free for students who wish to go on to high school. While the cost is not large by Canadian or American standards, it is nonetheless beyond many families' ability to pay. This is one way my wife and I chose to get involved in our community—by putting some of our neighbor kids through high school. It's a way of making a substantial difference in their prospects, and it is 100% cost-effective because it involves exactly zero administrative overhead. You simply pay for their tuition and uniform bills when they come due twice a year. When I paid these invoices I was always reminded of some business dealings I had in the early nineties with the head of a well-known charitable agency in a town where I lived in the States, one with a population of a quarter of a million. He was at that time making a salary well into six figures.

We recently sold our house in San Miguel and moved about a twenty-minute drive out into the country. We prefer that the parties and fiestas should be more optional, even if we can no longer walk to the plaza in *el centro*. We have heard enough fireworks to last us for a while. Our attitude has become a bit like the way we felt about snow when we left Minnesota. We didn't wish to preserve a sample, since if we ever wanted to recall exactly what it looked like as it piled up outside our windows while the furnace hummed in high gear, we could always watch it on TV. It can be really attractive from a distance.

So have we then walked away from an essential feature of Mexican culture? Not if we can recover it at any time with a twenty-minute trip to town. All expatriates who come here select those things, whether consciously or unconsciously, that they are interested in and wish to be involved with. No matter how long we live here, we can never become Mexicans except on paper, and we will always choose our connections to this culture from among our established interests and add to them from our new discoveries.

Has San Miguel been ruined by its own success? I doubt it. There's nothing wrong with it that better urban planning and a city government more committed to the public interest can't fix. There is also the question of whether the city's priorities ought to be more focused on tourists or residents. But like many things in México, achieving a rational balance that works for both may take a while.

So, having taken a few shots at things that need improvement, let's move on to what makes this place such a rewarding slice of Mexican life.

CHAPTER FIVE
TWO MARKETS

Shopping in San Miguel, and throughout most of México, is different than it is in the U.S. and Canada, although it more closely resembles shopping in many other places in the world that do not possess fully developed industrial economies. While San Miguel has two large supermarkets that are both now affiliated with the same national chain; a department store, also a chain member; and an Office Depot—an important asset to writers, as well as architects, office managers, and anyone else depending on up to date business equipment and supplies—most of the daily shopping remains personal and much smaller in scale.

The mere fact that not everyone here owns a refrigerator is a key factor in grocery shopping, but far from the only one. It means that many people buy their food nearly every day, on the day they plan to use it. There is also a longstanding preference for freshness over preservation and processing, a feeling that persists as well among owners of the most advanced refrigerators, even if it originates among those who own none. This is a more traditional society than we would find in either the U.S. or Canada. Change is not automatically viewed as improvement, nor is it welcomed for its own sake.

My wife and I tend to be locavores whenever possible. The definition of this term is that we prefer to eat food grown in this geographic region, although the reality is even more intimate, that we mostly eat the produce from the surrounding ten or fifteen kilometers. The Bajío, the name of this region, is an agricultural basin in the mountains and we live at 6400 feet.

Here a milk truck means a rather battered pickup with a dozen or so old-fashioned milk cans in the back held upright by a bungee cord. The big ladle on a hook nearby doesn't get washed between uses. The product it sells door to door is unrefrigerated, unpasteurized, unhomogenized, and unrepentant. It's just raw milk, direct from the cow that morning, and if you buy it that way on your doorstep, as people probably have for hundreds of years without the pickup, you will drink it that day, at room temperature, until it's gone. I don't drink it that way on any day, but many people do and live on to die cheerfully at an advanced age from other causes.

The Saturday Organic Market

Organic gardening and farming has been around for generations, but after its explosion as a widespread ideological and political movement in the sixties, its popularity continues to grow. People of the sixties generation will recall its prominence in venues like Stewart Brand's *The Whole Earth Catalogue*.

In response to the widespread preference for organically grown foods among both the expats and the natives here, many of whom still recall that era well, there is TOSMA (Tianguis Orgánica San Miguel de Allende), the Saturday morning organic market. It now operates in a famous dark red two story former hardware store building on the Ancha de San Antonio, whose original business (the Don Pedro Hardware) has now moved further up the street on the road to Celaya. The market is much closer in, near the intersection of Calle Stirling Dickinson.

Here in a covered multilayered space the vendors display a wide range of products anchored on local produce, but including ground and whole bean coffee from Chiapas, weaving from Oaxaca, and a breakfast and brunch row that offers food and music for the early part of the day. It's a rubbing elbows kind of place, one where you can reconnect with the friends you haven't seen for a couple of weeks, and others you'd rather wait a few weeks more before seeing again. As a smaller population within a small city, this gringo community has its ongoing squabbles, often political, and unfortunately it has inherited some of the uncivil behavior that Americans usually exhibit more on their own turf. In these times this is unfortunate, but probably unavoidable. In that sense, it still feels to me like a real community, one with a group of cousins that doesn't always get along. This sense of imperfect blending is, in a convoluted way, what this town is about. Perfect harmony can be dull and it never was either the goal or the process here.

A question lingers about how truly organic this market is in every case. As with any standards of purity, results can vary. Many vendors are strong supporters of the organic movement and display their certification. What we know is that the food is quite fresh and relatively untampered with. The Bajío, the large mountain-bound agricultural basin where San Miguel is located, has always been the most important farming area of Central México. Another aspect of this kind of market is that it offers people that wish to be locavores an opportunity to do so regularly. Many people prefer eating food that is locally grown, often practically within sight of the city. The kind of harvesting and preparation issues involved in bringing food in by semi trailer from two thousand miles away don't arise when the food is picked that morning three kilometers from where you buy it and four from where you eat it.

Recently more handcrafted products, mostly weaving and clothing, have joined this mixture, and it feels more and more like a genuine village market in the old style, but one still aimed at serving the tastes and needs of both Mexicans and expats alike. Usually a couple of strolling musicians work the crowd or set up in front of the brunch tables. The performance quality varies but the shoppers seem to enjoy them. The scene has already developed a depth of both patina and character.

In most cases the seasonality of local produce is truly reflected in the offerings. As I write this in January, the tomatoes are starting to fade off their best run, and some resemble refugees from a harsher environment, often scarred by an unpitying upbringing. The squash have had a great season and are still holding well, while the lettuce is returning with vigor. The carrots, sheltered from the weather in their quiet boroughs, are their consistent selves. Since we keep a horse, the quality of the carrots is always an issue to the whole family.

After its Saturday run, the lower rear section of the market building reverts to a parking area. But upstairs on several more levels, small shops and vendors offer a variety of other products throughout the week. Artisanal cheeses, either from cows or goats, bakery products, farm-made yogurts; all have changed our diet. Potatoes worthy of baking often appear, something not always available here in the past.

Even back in Minnesota we did not consume a lot of pre-prepared foods. Here it's even easier to continue that trend. This is a country where much of the population cannot afford heavily processed groceries. In the States what was always politely called the "value added" feature of heavy processing often makes the basic product too pricey for working people. Naturally, we tend to cook and plan meals based on available products. Wasn't this always the way it was before we became slaves of *convenience*? That was such a breakthrough word when I was growing up. It was magical. No one below the upper class had seen it before. Now it's lost its cachet because we know what making them convenient does to many raw food products.

If this sounds like ideology to some, that's not a profound concern for me. It's only a commonsense lifestyle. Our neighbors grow food nearby without pesticides or herbicides, and they sell it locally to residents who enjoy eating their food closer to is source. Although some support it for reasons of principle, the utilitarian in me supports it because it works so well as an easy and sensible way to live; one that seems honest, more wholesome, and respectful of the soil and the people who work it. We know personally many of the people who grow our food, and Monsanto is not welcome here, even under its new German name, Bayer.

Although it's less than seven years old, and in its second location, this market exudes the feeling of having evolved *organically* into a genuine entity, a vital and necessary part of the larger community. I use the word here in the sense of starting out as a planned venture that has been taken over by its vendors and customers, and as it matured became essential to the public. In that sense it has triumphantly outgrown its plan. You only have to walk in from the street on a Saturday morning to experience the rhythm and vigor of its life.

The Tuesday Market

Like a shimmering mirage that lasts only until your next blink, the Tuesday Market (Tianguis) appears once a week at dawn, assembled upon a vast windswept concrete slab near the parking lot of the San Miguel municipal sports complex, off the Querétaro highway. Just as quickly it evaporates after sunset. Each week, from battered pickups and vans, a hoard of Hispanic merchant Bedouins conjures up an entire world of itinerant economics almost from thin air.

Once assembled, the market is screened on the sides with brilliant tarps of red and blue and yellow, putting a bold face on what I used to think when I first arrived was desperation commerce. But that was neither fair nor objective, and it revealed more about my ignorance than it did about my insights that early on. It was the untutored observation of a newcomer, and later I understood that to the locals, retailing is simply divided a few degrees further and more minutely than north of the border, reflecting both the scarcity of capital and the intensity of labor at the base of the economic pyramid. While a great deal of the merchandise is new, reuse is also an active value. After I'd lived in San Miguel for a few years I realized that the Tuesday Market, rather than being a low rent sideline, was closer to being the economic heartbeat of the city.

My wife dragged me through again and again until I started buying my shirts there for eighty pesos, or superb Oaxaca cheese—with an authenticity usually unavailable anywhere except in Oaxaca—for less than two dollars a pound. The shrimp is fresher and half the price of those at the supermarket. The octopus looks like it might reach out and grab your fingers as you pass, so keep your hands in your pockets. You can buy fresh chicken breasts boned and pounded, ready to stuff with spinach and cheese and roll up for a quick sauté. There are also rows of skinned frogs whose eyes still bulge with surprise at their fate, but I always pass on those.

Poles inside the market support other bright coverings that shelter most of the interior from the sun. Within, long rows of tables display all the new or slightly tattered goods that won't support the overhead of a bricks and mortar store. Racks of used shoes are extremely inexpensive, and they cost only slightly more if you need them to match. Piles of pre-worn clothing, bins of carefully pounded out used nails, buckets of screws of mixed sizes. For them I think the unit of measure should not be a quarter pound or a half-kilo, it ought to be a *diversity* of screws.

Next come sets of rusty horseshoes, probably no more than three of a given size. The discontinued currency, both in bills and coins, always fascinates me. More of the money in México has been devalued than not. Some of the great fortunes of the past can be bought there in piles and stacks atop battered wooden tables for a few hundred current pesos, much like the failed dreams of overthrown regimes. I enjoy picking up these historic banknotes and flipping through them, the grubby shopworn faces of mustachioed dictators and Aztec chieftains. Between my palms they offer the texture of wilted history.

Several tables are stacked with CDs and DVDs, all of them bootlegged. I don't think I've ever seen a genuinely issued one for sale here, other than in the Liverpool department store. A tall pegboard displays a dozen new backpacks, as fresh as last year's hottest trend. Here's a full range of remote control units; who would know which one to buy? And food stalls, offering heaps of stuff that you'd think would reduce any gringo to gastric distress within five minutes, yet tables full of them are happily eating here. Ah, México! Parental discretion advised. A man passes with buckets of garlic bulbs draped from his shoulders, yelling *ocho por diez*, eight of them for ten pesos; fifty-two U.S. cents.

There are literally tools by the ton. Got a plumbing project that needs a quarter acre of wrenches? Imagine loading up 300 square feet of sledge hammers, axes, pry bars, anvils and used circular saw blades and hauling them away to be unloaded again the following day in a neighboring town, because the Tuesday Market is only called that in San Miguel. It's the Wednesday Market tomorrow in Celaya or Salamanca, or in points unknown further down the road. This gypsy mercantile life is one of unceasing movement, of engagement and reengagement. It is every day's pop-up market, somewhere and everywhere.

This roving circuit is part of an ancient tradition, reaching back to any time or town in medieval Europe or colonial America, North or South, when it was relatively safe to travel. Only war or the plague could shut it down for long. The market fairs on Sundays, the religious feast day fairs, the harvest markets in the fall—these were all forerunners of our Tuesday Market in today's San Miguel. No bricks and mortar establishments were required, and not much capital (since little was ever available). Some few meters of faded fabric for sunshade and to shed rainfall, with a few poles to brace it against the sky, this was all it took to open for business. The overhead of these nomadic retailers was mainly time, labor, enough feed on hand, and water or grazing resources in barren places to keep the mules and horse drawn wagons plodding from town to town.

As I walked through the crowded stalls it suddenly occurred to me that this absence of capital, so common in México, is a great preserver of old folkways and lifestyles. Of course there is much operating capital and enormous wealth in this country—it's just not widely distributed. Great care is taken to keep those piles intact, until that time when they emerge devalued in dog-eared stacks at the other end of this market.

I paused before a wall of strawberries formed like a perfectly scaled medieval fortress that only lacked a drawbridge. Inside, a woman was confined on three sides by an eighteen-inch bank of berries, all about the same size and all facing the same direction, pointed bottoms out. Some assembly is required, I thought. She was doing a fabulous business. I couldn't help buying half a kilo myself for ten pesos.

The next stall displayed three walls of sports jerseys. My eye was caught by the team name most repeated on them, *Bimbo*. Neither a lifestyle choice nor an epithet this time, Bimbo, México's largest bakery company, is the sponsor of several *fútbol* teams. They make the equivalent of Wonder Bread. Teenaged American tourists snap up these shirts by the hundreds. The proprietor offered to pull one down in my size, but I shook my head. *Los Escritores* would be my team, I said to him, The Authors.

He only shook his head as I moved on.

At the far end I found my favorite clothing stall, one where I had once paid the peso equivalent of eight dollars for a brand new silk Tommy Bahama shirt with all the tags intact. A hundred and twenty bucks in the States, I recall thinking at that moment. I've since worn it more than half a dozen times at public readings and book signings. Seven or eight other shirts from this vendor are also part of my regular wardrobe. Back home I could never have imagined shopping like this. The lesson is that it's good to be ready to change in ways you did not anticipate.

A mild note of caution is in order about this market. Particularly during holidays and fiestas, when San Miguel swells with tourists and vacationers, people of questionable character come to town as well, usually seeking pickpocket opportunities in markets like this. Bring with you only what you need, not six credits cards, your driver's license and passport, and the only existing copy of your visa. Purses are obvious targets, as are backpacks that are easily slit from the bottom while you are distracted.

I don't say it's a tough town, but using reasonable caution anywhere is wise. The walking around money in your wallet or purse can be three weeks pay at hard labor for the person in line behind you.

I've often said that it's hard to know exactly what

you're looking at in México. The Tuesday Market is a perfect example. It's taken my gringo eyes a while to get used to it. It's a way of life as much as a particular place, a transient style of doing business that is still both intimate and friendly, and above all, personal. And that personal aspect is one of those qualities about Mexican business and society that pleases me constantly on a daily basis. It's a sustaining feature, and as I write this, we have been here for eleven years and counting.

Other Markets

Of course the Tuesday Market and the Organic Market are not the only ones in San Miguel. Also worth a visit is the Artisan Market in el centro. Situated along a single sunken street between the far end of Calle Hidalgo moving north toward the Mercado Ramirez for about three blocks, it offers a different ambience and style than the other markets, although their products overlap in some areas.

For one thing, it is like a tunnel with no roof, set below the level of the surrounding streets and houses as if it were once a watercourse running from high to low. It's a promenade with no lateral venues. You walk through glancing from side to side until something catches your fancy. The day I returned to examine it for this piece, it was not crowded.

You will also want to take a look at the Mercado Ramirez downtown, and the San Juan de Dios market on Calle Indio Triste, the street of the Sad Indian. The Mercado Rural in the Guadalupe Neighborhood, held in the first Sunday of every month. A visit to any of them is worth the time, since each is unique in character and deserves a closer look.

CHAPTER SIX
COUNTRY LIFE

In the United States I resided five years in California, fifty-eight years in Minnesota, and I never imagined I would end up living on the edge of a small village in the mountains of central México. I had always thought I'd come to earth in Italy or the south of France, both of which I knew from numerous visits. It was not hard to imagine either of those places as home.

They are both, however, pricey areas to live in and the dollar is not well respected there. Before I moved to México I had little knowledge of Latin America. My only experience with this country was an afternoon I spent in Tijuana in the summer of 1963. As far as I knew more recently, the place had fallen away because of tectonic plate issues and the continent now stopped at Laredo. As far as what mattered, it was all water from there to Antarctica, and I have never been a boat person.

As I write this today, I've been living just outside of San Miguel for about a bit more than a year. It's a quiet place during the week, but on weekends people come from all over the country on individual or collective pilgrimages to our local religious shrine.

While my neighborhood is San Miguelito, the adjacent village is called Atotonilco, and my house is twenty minutes from San Miguel. This area offers a cluster of hot springs, and judging from the archaeological remains, it was important to the indigenous people for centuries before the arrival of the first Spanish settlers early in the 1540s.

As was its practice throughout Latin America, the Catholic Church took over sites that were already sacred to the indigenous peoples and reconsecrated them for its own purposes, often combining a saint's name with the local title. In the first half of the eighteenth century the Church built a sanctuary in Atotonilco dedicated to Jesus of Nazareth. The ruined arches of a cloister are still attached to it. I suppose the style of the architecture could be called regional late Baroque, and of course, it's reputed to be the scene of many miraculous cures.

In addition, the local (and national) hero of the War of Independence, Ignacio Allende, a San Miguel de Allende native (then known as San Miguel el Grande), was married there in 1793. In 1810 as an army commander, he led his body of troops in revolt against Spain. They traveled the sixteen kilometers to Atotonilco where they joined forces with Father Miguel Hidalgo from the nearby town of Dolores (later Dolores Hidalgo) who had led his seven or eight thousand Indian followers, armed with whatever they could summon as weapons on short notice, to the meeting. From inside the church, they took the local copy of the painting of the Lady of Guadalupe down from the wall, attached it to a pole, and used it as a battle standard. Then they traveled into San Miguel, where with the aid of the Aldama brothers and some other *insurgentes*, they announced the birth of the nation of México from the old city hall that still overlooks the plaza. What a moment!

That divine standard did not help them to prevail against the overwhelming Spanish colonial forces, however, and the two pioneer leaders, Hidalgo and Allende, were both dead by June of 1811. But as in many similar situations, they were as valuable to their cause as dead heroes as they had ever been as living leaders. It was not until Father José Morelos joined the rebellion that the rebels began to win some battles.

On the three or four times a week when I drive past that sanctuary I can see them again gathered there on that unique day in September of 1810, with their standards and rifles and lances lifted in anger and naive readiness.

I live upstream at a sweet spot on a sharp turn of the Río Laja, only a little more than a kilometer from that square in front of the church.

Our house is built in the Santa Fe style, adobe in appearance, and now well weathered. The side that fronts the valley is mostly glass, so the views from the room where I'm writing this book go on forever in the morning light. Each dawn is different. We are situated on more than two and a half acres, so our neighbors on this side of the river (we can see only one from inside the house) are within waving distance, but too far away to have a conversation without yelling, and living here, we have found little to yell about anymore. This is the antithesis of our situation in town, where like everyone else, we were close enough to shake hands with our neighbors over the wall.

The sounds here are much different. There is a crew of dogs in the nearby hamlet of San Miguelito that starts to respond to the awakening chickens around five-thirty. Knowing them well, the chickens put up with little interference as they begin their daily soil scan. They are truly free range. The sheep wake up about the same time, and the goats, a few minutes later. None are close enough to disturb us. Now I am wondering if there is anything out here to disturb us. We could surely do it to ourselves, were we so inclined, but the surrounding terrain offers nothing but the population that was already here on our arrival. When the figs come out in droves on the tree near our kitchen door we share them with the birds. There is enough for everyone.

The insect life is far more diverse than in town. The large cockroaches that emerge from the sewers there in hot weather we have not seen out here so far, although we've killed seven scorpions in the house. These are not the smaller pale ones that are so poisonous; they're the larger dark reddish brown version whose sting is milder. In any case, their sinister look wins them no friends. I have heard that you can reach under your pillow and discover one in your hand, but we never have.

Some time back, the five-foot long black king snake did not look up at me as he passed a meter beyond my desk on the other side of the windows. A little research told me he prefers not to bite any of us as he hunts down small rodents in the night.

Since I returned to my writing career, over the last thirteen years as I produced thirty-two books—this is number thirty-three—I've worked in both chaos and calm. I know I can manage to write in either condition, but I greatly prefer calm, and that is the feature that drew us most to this place. In the yard fronting the house beyond the mature fig tree, we have nearly a hundred olives. The garden is full of lavender and roses. I began to sense early on that this place possesses a unique spirit, although I could not have said for a while what or who it might be.

When we arrived I had two of my Paul Zacher mysteries (#19 and #20) about 85% finished, and another one that had defied me for years stalled at 70%. In seven months I finished all three of those, and started another and finished that one as well. Clearly, this setting has its own creative muse. I feel like I am combining forces with something I have never encountered before and could not define.

Some people around us are crushed by poverty and others top heavy with affluence. Our neighbor directly across the valley is a very wealthy Mexican who sometimes comes and goes by helicopter from his main home in Mexico City. My wife's horse, Martina, boards at a ranch just five minutes away. She had a walk-on part in Uneasy Rider that she has never forgotten. I believe it went to her head. From the thorny mesquite trees here we pick the pale seed pods and feed them to her. She believes they are candy.

Always present before us in the valley is the river. For between six and eight months of the year the Río Laja, as it passes below our house on the bluff, is dry. You can walk the length of it in the center of the riverbed and not get the soles of your shoes wet.

When the rainy season begins in June puddles form here and there, tentative, appearing to be uncertain of their permanence. Most dry up soon and disappear.

When we descend from the plateau above the valley, we skirt the edge through the village of San Miguelito, a street of poor houses and shops with million dollar views on the valley side. Down the slope waits a bridge, the only local route across the intermittent river.

It's truly a simple affair at a shady bend. People who read these things would say it offers a good vibe. A single lane provides passage for a single car. A single person may walk carefully next to it, but that is all. Any vehicle approaching from the other direction waits for its turn. Its weary surface is weathered unembellished concrete. No rails are provided. The drop to the river bottom is no more than four or five feet. Its severe simplicity makes the Depression-era WPA constructions in the States appear extravagant and ornate. Below, a double arch supports its span of about twenty-five or thirty feet.

As the rainy season develops and the creek fills and widens, the locals sweep the upstream side of the bridge free of floating debris: tree branches, fragments of lumber, brush that's been lifted loose from its moorings along the banks.

The local people, many of whom work in the nearby village of Atotonilco a hundred meters away, depend on that bridge to get to their jobs or to religious services at the historic Santuario. Later in the season vigorous currents develop and the water will begin to flow over the surface of the bridge. The locals will continue to cross unconcerned, carrying their shoes. I keep using it until I can no longer see the edges of the concrete. Only the current suggests where it is, or even was. Some things in life can be implicit or hypothetical; bridges cannot.

In the last week of September, it is the end of

the rainy season, usually winding up with some heavy downpours. The Río Laja has grown swollen and aggressive, even hostile. What was once a dry track picking its way through the emerald woods has become a brownish green estuary plucking at the hillsides, swirling among the trees. Like a miniature Nile, it rushes on full of silted minerals and decayed organic matter. It forgives no miscalculations.

Today when I walked down the road toward the village, the bridge had disappeared without a trace. Getting to work and to school for those on the west side of the seasonal river is now impossible for the ones who don't have a car and the disposable time to drive downriver to cross on a different bridge.

I believe our bridge is still down there somewhere, out of sight beneath the turbulent brown water. The once dry creek is now about eighty feet across. This means it's running six or seven feet deep over the bridge.

The next bridge downriver is a much higher and more serious affair eight kilometers to the south over rutted and washboard dirt roads. I don't know how people manage this. I'm sure it looks to them like fate, which is the cause of most things here, good or bad.

This is a typical feature of country life here in Central México. Some things work and some don't, but few things work all the time. While it is obvious that a taller bridge would change people's lives, the idea that government will do something about it is not one you ever hear. Nature is a feature of existence, a system created by a Christian God with his own purposes, and it may even border on the sacrilegious to try and change the role that the river and the bridge play in people's lives. It has its own rhythm, and things mostly go on here in the Laja Valley as they always have.

I know we will get by here in our house on the bluff, and more than get by. In fact, we will flourish. In this tiny enclave some of our neighbors are enormously creative people. This neglected house is coming together and we have nearly gotten everything up and running. It had not been lived in for a while and needed more than a little attention. As I wrote earlier, I never thought I would end up in a place like this, but serendipity is a powerful, if subtle force. I would never try to ignore it.

Since we were told by our neighbors that this pattern was the norm, as I finished writing this chapter, I had no idea at all of what was to come in the following season.

CHAPTER SEVEN
A MONTH IN HIGH SUMMER

In the previous chapter I wrote about one season on the local river, the Río Laja, which passes below our bluff-side home about a hundred feet below. I am returning to it now in a somewhat different state of mind. As I said earlier, eight months of the year it's dry. You can literally walk the center of the streambed and not get your shoe soles damp.

We live in a small, gated enclave of nineteen properties on about sixty acres. The owners are divided between Mexicans and Americans. Only eight homes have been built there, so we feel very much out in the country. Our lot is typical in size, between two and a half and three acres.

I want to revisit that small, single-lane concrete bridge that links us with the pilgrimage village of Atotonilco. Normally, in mid July that bridge disappears below the water level and reappears about six weeks later, as it so predictably did above. We had been watching this for years before we moved out here, and last year was typical.

Now it is nine months after I wrote that earlier chapter—books take a while to write and they're not often written in the order they appear. May is always the hottest month, and this year it was hotter than normal. Some welcome rain appeared the first week of June and within a couple of days puddles had formed in the riverbed. We'd had too little in the first five months of the year, and it was starting to look like a drought. I'd had to water our olive orchard and fig tree in cycles. Then quite abruptly, the rains began in earnest.

Traditionally the rainy season, June to September, brings us an hour or so of rain three or four times a week in the late afternoon. In town you can sit it out at a delayed lunch and watch the locals pass wearing large plastic bags over their heads with a hole cut out for the face. The more upscale ones have umbrellas, which are normally used here more to ward off the sun.

On the sixth of June we approached the bridge and pulled over to allow a pickup to cross from the other side. At this point we could no longer see the bridge, we could only infer its location by the currents in the water swiftly passing over it. The left edge, the upstream side, was defined by a dense tangle of debris, mainly branches and uprooted weeds, that had accumulated against it. A slight drop in water level suggested where the right side was. Normally around eight feet wide between dry and wet seasons, now the river was about forty feet wide there, the color of mud and equally as opaque.

I studied the pickup as it drew nearer. As it came toward us the water did not quite reach the underside of the vehicle so I decided to chance it too. I was reluctant to start to float and lose traction because of it. Off the bridge the water was only about four or five feet deep, although the current was swift. I waved at the driver as he passed and then pulled onto the place where I knew the apron of the bridge began.

Immediately I felt the pressure of the rushing water on the wheels. It arced away in an angular wave. We just put on a fierce grin and cruised across. Pulling up onto the slippery rock strewn shore beyond I had the feeling that it would be a while before we went that way again. After all, we could still get to town on the road going north from the hamlet of Cieneguita. That would be our back way home. Stretches of it were rough and pitted, but it was open, even though it also ran along a lower part of the Río Laja.

In the days that followed, what was soon clear was that the weather pattern had changed dramatically from normal. We began getting vicious storms that dropped huge volumes of water overnight. Before the house, down in the valley, the river grew rapidly. It was soon about 150 feet wide. From upstream, to the north, swirling trains of debris rushed by, following a serpentine course through the current. The surge in volume was even more about what was happening upriver than the rain we were getting, massive as it was. I remarked to my wife several times how fortunate we were that the power had not gone out. As we had learned over the years, the ability of the electric company to consistently deliver its product can be chancy, and rain was often part of the reason.

By the middle of June the water was tracking up the road on the opposite side of the valley. The new islands had disappeared. Dozens of mature trees were standing isolated far out in the stream. The tiny Río Laja, usually dry, was now about 300 feet wide. From our viewpoint at the top of the bluff, the entire valley was nearly covered. In the midst of a thunderous down-pour at the end of the week we had a power outage that lasted less than ten hours. We felt fortunate when it came back on. From not far away, I had heard an explosion in the night, and in the morning we saw that a branch had fallen on the road along the edge of the valley and taken a transformer down with it. We kept telling ourselves this was a record-breaking year, but we didn't feel lucky to be witnessing it.

Halfway through the last week of June, our third solid week of punishing weather, I awakened at two AM after another double explosion. The power went out im-mediately. The rain was only moderate. In the morning within our enclave of eight houses, none had any power.

When dawn arrived at about 6:30 I extinguished the candles. The Laja was now about 450 feet wide and rushing past with an audibly triumphant tone. Within my field of view six huge mature trees had been undermined and fallen forward into the water.

At ten in the morning I walked down to the gate and talked to our gatekeeper. The electric company had come quickly after he called them at eight. Following a survey of the scene they gave him the bad news. The pole that had been damaged was thirty feet into the water, which was shallow there, but it needed to be approached from the opposite side, since the slope on ours was too steep to navigate with their equipment. It was too dangerous to attempt a repair until the water receded and the road was exposed and passable. Although they had already left, I could imagine the Mexican shrug that accompanied this withdrawal.

And in a larger sense, I also knew right away what this meant. Our normal return to manageable waters happened at the start of September, nine or ten weeks away. But with the volume we'd have by then, many times normal, how long would that take to disperse and normalize in our part of the valley below? Sadly, I hummed a few bars of *Old Man River* as I walked back. *Cause he just keeps rollin' He keeps rollin' along.*

Back in the house I surveyed the remaining battery strength on my laptop and my wife's iPhone. We could still get Internet at that point, through her iPhone hotspot, because our Internet server was down. But of course there was no way to recharge either device except by leaving home.

Our main route to town was via the Dolores Hidalgo highway, but that was blocked because the bridge was probably twelve feet underwater. Our backup route, to the west and down toward and through the village of Cieneguita, had been, as we discovered online, just recently closed by the army because of flooding and landslides. A causeway style bridge on the road that led from it to the highway to the airport had been undermined and collapsed. A third way offered a four-kilometer stretch of dreadfully rutted dirt road that extended the trip to town from twenty minutes to an hour as it threatened to break your axles.

During the night we had transferred almost everything from the refrigerator into the freezer, which was still cold but not frozen. For lunch we wolfed down all the deli meats we could stand. As we ate we had a grim discussion of our options. It was simply not possible to live in the house without power. The cost of renting a hotel room or a bed and breakfast for the months the power would take to return was prohibitive. And what would we do with the dog during that time?

"Although it still feels like home, I'm beginning to feel there's a fragile quality to living here," I said to

Kristine, my wife. "The Mexican countryside is beautiful, scenic, exotic, but it's not always your friend."

"We can fix that," she said, putting on a cheerful look. "Let's rent a generator until the power comes back on. How much could that cost?"

I saw at once that this was the only answer. Without it we had no communications, no refrigeration, and no water, since our well is served by an electric pump. We would've been compelled to live by candlelight in a style the Victorians would've thought impoverished. I'd only be able to write as long as my laptop battery had power. My only other option would be to dictate into a tiny battery-power voice recorder I've been using for the interviews in this book.

A call to our contractor got the process in motion. Two hours later, she called back to say she had found several for rent, but none were available for eleven days. They would cost forty dollars a day. What! I covered the phone with my hand while I sputtered.

Still, considering the costs of camping out in some hostelry without most of our stuff while we boarded the dog, it still seemed justifiable, if not entirely reasonable. "What if we bought one?" I said.

She had anticipated this. "They cost 25,000 pesos." On that day, that meant about $1,300 U.S. I ran some quick math. If we rented one for only a month, it would be $1,200 or so. If we rented it for two months,

$2,400. It made more sense to buy one, because once we were finished with it we could offer a nearly new generator for sale for $1,000, a nice discount, and we'd only be out about $300 for using it for a month or more. It would be ready for pickup in the morning and could be up and running by lunchtime. We'd be able to shower. We could take the rough and tumble back road and go buy new provisions for the refrigerator. We gave her the go-ahead. By then it was about five o'clock. We gave each other a high five, knowing we had solved a nasty problem by owning it ourselves. Proactive was the term that came to mind.

We had never felt we could depend on organizations like the utility companies, the police, or other support groups to the same degree we had in the States. That was no more than the reality of living in México. This is a country that relies more on family and community when in need.

The electric company had made it clear that they planned to do nothing until the water level went down to nearly normal. It was too dangerous and we were just out of luck. Like many similar unfortunate events, it may have been fate that was responsible. I felt like asking why they had placed the pole in a location where it might reasonably be expected to be encroached upon by seasonal rains. But I already knew the answer. They were better at dealing with reality than possibility. For most of them, planning for unlikely events was not part of their job. They had originally placed the pole on dry land and now it wasn't. That was all. It was the land that had moved, not the pole. I could not deny this.

I was still feeling quite satisfied with the efficient way we'd handled that dilemma when the power came back on without warning at seven o'clock. I think we both nearly fell over. There was no possibility that we could've come up with that was more remote.

When I saw our gate guard the next morning he told me that the electric crew had come back un-announced in the late afternoon, discovered the steep, rocky goat trail outside the corner of the property wall, and headed on down to fix the problem.

I included this rather twisted narrative as a fol-low up to the earlier bridge chapter because it illustrates several important features of living in México.

One of them would have to be unpredictabil-ity. People like our electrical repair crew would not see any need to announce their intentions to return if they didn't have to come into your house. Quite properly, they would expect you to be grateful that they returned at all. But if you have felt, as we did, the strong need to act unilaterally to solve a problem that would soon devastate your lifestyle if unaddressed, one they have by their own admission bailed on, then you can be vulnerable to the changes in plan they bring about by altering their intentions.

Another feature would be resilience. Most expats who emigrate to México are retired. I know from numerous conversations in this book and others I've written on expat life, that the meaning of that term varies widely. But whatever retirement means, it must also include this feature to work well: it's that what it cannot mean is simply kicking back and coasting with no awareness of your surroundings. We do see this happen here, partly because the cost of living is a bargain relative to the States. Do your homework on your destination town, since this is not Cleveland, Anaheim, or Poughkeepsie. Most of your instinctive assumptions will be wrong, especially when they represent what you would most like to think. I have illustrated myself above as a long time resident making wrong decisions in a tough situation for the very best and most carefully conceived of reasons. It is a true story and a process that you can also anticipate happening to you in one form or another. Fortunately, our contractor was able to cancel the order for the generator even though the seller had started to assemble it for shipping to us.

With their long life experience, people in the typical expat age group do not like to be wrong. I'm of retirement age myself, even though I could never retire from my writing life because I'm having more fun than I ever did with the other careers I've had. Nonetheless, it's not foolish to imagine how well your life experience will apply here, and it often does. People are people anywhere. The problem is that it still happens less often that way than it would have at home. I actually welcome being wrong (occasionally), not because I like to appear stupid or naive, but because I always learn something when I do. So I make a point of taking chances that I might well not have taken in Minneapolis, where we lived until we sold everything and left in 2007. Some of this is clearly about risk tolerance and its role in learning, and that is the fundamental point of this chapter. There are times when you are simply not going to get it right, no matter how well you have applied every single lesson that life ever taught you. If you can absorb that fact by reading this chapter, and stay flexible and undefeated, you will be well ahead of the game. Far ahead of where I was when I got off that plane eleven years ago.

CHAPTER EIGHT
THE AMBIENCE OF MOTION

So what to do in México once you arrive? You've finished unpacking, you've got your utilities connected, and your refrigerator is stocked. The beer is cold. You've met some of your neighbors and they seem at least plausible. One of them even brought you a bottle of local wine as a housewarming present. This is followed by a slight pause. Of course you already knew what to do to occupy yourself back in Fort Worth or Fort Wayne, but is there anything to do in a small city called San Miguel up in the mountains in the center of México besides watch the jacaranda bloom and the jalapeños grow? The actuality of what you have done starts to settle over you. Now you have to make it real and you're not quite sure what that means. You decide to take the question in small bites, even though you know at one level that it really means you need to make a whole new life.

There is of course cable television, offering approximately the same mix of channels you had at home. But TV can be a watery kind of sustenance for a hungry mind, a bowl of gruel when you want a platter of steak, and anyway, you didn't leave the States to be a couch potato. There's a movie complex at the mall that delivers a mix of Mexican and U.S. films with subtitles in English when filmed in Spanish and vice versa. That's all very good, but it's not enough to keep you going.

On impulse I pulled out our weekly bilingual newspaper, *Atención*, which appears on Fridays. It offers a pullout section called *Que Pasa*, or, What's happening in the coming week. Here's a random cull from what's offered in the larger ads. At the charmingly restored Angela Peralta Theater a quartet is doing a show called Masterpieces of the Jazz. The next page brings us a day trip tour to the monarch butterfly preserve in the neighboring state of Michoacán. A photography exhibit at a downtown art gallery. A major 30% off sale at the Liverpool department store. Maria Sanchéz is doing a concert featuring Brazilian music on Tuesday. Handily enough, the centerfold of that section is a detailed city map.

On Friday a vineyard tour includes a visit to the attractive nearby town of Bernal, which possesses one of he world's largest monoliths. On Tuesday there's a tour of several local classic haciendas. They are probably from the eighteenth or even seventeenth century. These are just the events that bought display ads. But densely packed around them are entire categories of mostly ongoing activities that appeal to a broad range of interests. This section is called *The Calendar*, and arranged day by day, it appears in both English and Spanish. In no particular order, an entire run of concerts, gallery openings, restaurant special occasions (many with entertainment), bird walks, book sales, bridge games, a ballet presentation, a book signing by a world-famous chef, the Rotary Meeting, the Hanukkah Party at the Jewish Community and Cultural Center, the weekly House and Garden Tour. Many, many others, but let me catch my breath. I have barely skimmed this list.

Then there are the community meetings and tutorials. Four different art workshops in this single week. Five language workshops. Four meditation and yoga meetings. Songwriting, tango, and scrabble gatherings. Bereavement groups, Lion's Club, laws of attraction, and a course in miracles. Hospice, knitting hats and scarves for kids in the countryside, an animal shelter tour. Catholic (of course) services, plus Quaker, Episcopalian, Unitarian Universalist, Jewish, and Mindfulness Practice at the Zen Center. Twelve-step programs every day of the week in different spots around town, including Women In Recovery and ACA, Adult Children of Alcoholics. This only scratches the surface.

I am tempted to suggest you shouldn't spend a lot of money on a house here because you'll never spend any time there. But it's good to have a home to be in, which is the focus of much of this book.

If I feel like taking a break from this whirlwind

of activity I can head down to *el centro*. There I will find the main square that fronts our grand so-called parish church, the Parroquia. This plaza is called the *jardín*. Under the ficus trees, which are sculpted into the form of hatboxes or kettledrums, the cast iron benches are laid out on the paths emanating from the bandstand. This is where the serious discussions about the state of the world occur. There sit the park bench philosophers from Toledo, Toronto, or Tallahassee, Duluth or Detroit, as they kick back and hash out those issues that rarely come up in Washington or Moscow, Paris or Beijing. Nor are these conversations ever given advance notice in the pages of *Que Pasa*, but they are nonetheless real and important.

Political conversations often occur there too, but many people have given that up because they're sick of them.

This urban square hosts a different kind of activity beyond the concert halls and restaurants, away from the bird walks and haciendas, the butterflies and the art walks. It's called thought and recollection, calm communication. While it burns far fewer calories than the hurly-burly above, it offers its own set of rewards.

Like everything else here, the choice, or the mix of choices, is yours. In the scattered list of published offerings above, none of them was titled *The List of Other People's Expectations You Must Fulfill*. While that list would be blank, the one titled *The List of Unforced Choices Before You* has too many pages to read at one sitting. Open it at random and you will nearly always find something to catch your fancy.

CHAPTER NINE
DEATH AND DYING

Whether expats or not, we are all travelers, and while our road maps are different, and each of the roads we travel through life is unique, they all end in the same place. This journey is exempt from denial or evasion, and our best policy is to be prepared for the day it happens. Although we all grasp the truth of this instinctively, not everyone can openly face it.

The law in México requires either burial or cremation within twenty-four hours. The unspoken reason for this is that embalming is not often practiced among poorer people—the majority of the population—so the timely disposal of the dead is a public health issue. Many wakes here begin within hours of the passing of the deceased, and continue through the night as processions of family and friends appear to pay their last respects. Often these rituals are held in a nearby garage to avoid the expense of a funeral director's parlor. At dawn the coffin is carried down the hill to the Panteón for burial on the shoulders of the mourners.

The Twenty-four Hour Association was founded to provide for a pre-arranged transition when the need arises. Through this organization the local residents, generally the expats, can make their wishes known and arrange for and prepay the fees for their interment or cremation. For those living without other family members in México this can be the best way to make their own final arrangements. Association affiliates can have a friend prepared to make the call, and the organization will take care of the rest.

Even if they arrived with a spouse, not everyone is still part of a couple here, so for people who die without any family in San Miguel, what will follow? Quite simply, their instructions filed with the Association will be promptly carried out, and their grand niece in Cincinnati or Sarasota will not be awakened in the middle of the night by someone who speaks no English and given four hours to respond when she's never in her life been out of the country and her minor in college was Swedish. She has never before had to distinguish between *lefse* and a tortilla. This is the ultimate definition of being blindsided.

This was the extent of what I knew before I decided to take a closer look at this issue. The existence of the Association is not as widely known as it ought to be, and I'm sure many people wonder what exactly will happen when they die here. As I often do when I need help, I sat down with a more knowledgeable person. In this case it was Natalie Hardy, who has been involved with the Association for seventeen years, as well as other NGOs, and she was quite happy to talk to me. We sat at the table in her second floor dining room. The nearby windows opened on a well of morning light.

"How did The Twenty-four Hour Association get started?"

"It was founded in 1965—which means we are in our fifty-third year now—by a retired navy admiral named Alex Charlton. A law existed then, and still does, that stated that one's remains had to be dealt with in twenty-four hours. Part of that was because embalming and cremation were not as commonly practiced then as they are today. Embalming was available an hour away in Celaya, and for cremation you had to go to Mexico City. Because of that there was no time to contact relatives of those that passed away on foreign soil and get them down here within that amount of time. The admiral decided to put together an organization that takes care of those matters for foreigners that have to deal with Mexican law in unfamiliar situations. He brought a few expatriates together at a meeting in the Instituto Allende and they assembled this group."

Natalie Hardy is a tall woman with dark hair and animated features. Listening to her command of the detail I couldn't help but feel people using the

Association were in good hands.

"How would a person set up a connection with the Association?"

"It's for members only, and the process is that you set up a file indicating who you wish contacted, and what you want done with your remains. Early in the history of the Association they buried people in the regular Panteón alongside the locals."

"How did your involvement start and what has your role become?"

"I came down here with my husband in 1999. It was the first time I came with him. We bought a house impulsively, as so many do." She paused to grin at this idea. "This was it for us for retirement, although we were both still working at that time. Shortly afterward he became ill. In 2002 he retired and we moved down here. He had ALS, and there was simply no hope for survival with that. We knew about the Twenty-four Hour Association from hearsay, because it keeps a low profile. We thought it would be a good idea to join on general principles. In 2004 he passed away."

"You were able to see very quickly how well it works."

"Yes, and I was amazed at how the Association took over for me. It was a good thing because I was in a nonfunctional state, something quite unanticipated for me. I was very grateful to them, and when I was invited to join the board, I did. I've had that position ever since. I am also the public relations director, and currently the vice president."

This was an added wrinkle I hadn't thought of. It was not only about people in the States struggling to deal with the long distance passing of their family members, it was also about your own spouse who may have seen your death coming, but might still be surprised and disabled in unexpected ways when that day arrived. We may think we're prepared, but we can never know how we'll react until that time comes.

"When a member dies, then the organization takes over and acts on these instructions that have been filed. This would have been prepaid, is that correct?"

"It must be completely prepaid."

"How much is the fee now?"

"There are two prices. One is for a simple crema-tion with the ashes strewn or whatever else you might want done with them. This currently costs $1,000. Burial options within the Panteón exist as well, where your ash-es can be put in a niche, where the body can be interred in the ground or in the wall with the niches. All of those choices are currently $1500."

"And I've seen that there is now a separate area set aside for expats."

"Absolutely, although it hasn't always been that way. In 1973 the municipality enlarged and improved the Panteón. They granted the Association about 1,000 square meters, and it's a beautiful piece of land. We paid something like 30,000 pesos in 1973 to put up the wall and make it ours." I had no way to calculate what value that might be in dollars this much later, and after two currency devaluations and constant less radical fluctuations.

"Is the Association primarily for people who live here alone, or is it popular with couples too?"

"It's a combination of both. My husband and I were a couple when we joined. Of course there are a lot of widowed people who have been part of a couple but no longer are."

And in any couple there will ultimately be only one survivor.

"What happens if the decedent wanted to be buried in the U. S. after he'd already joined the Association?"

"This is an NGO type of organization, so it's not for profit. Your money is refunded if your plans change. If you want to be buried in the U. S. as a member, we do not go any further than helping the relative or friends get the remains shipped up there."

"With the $1500 you pay to be buried here, is that in perpetuity? Do you own that plot in the soil?"

Natalie smiled. "It's yours in perpetuity. I hesitate to say you 'own' it in that we are dealing with México and I have seen many laws changed. Still, we have been going for more than fifty years and so far we've ridden with the changes. I have no reason to think it will shift in any major way."

"They don't dig you up at some point if your grandnephew in Bismarck hasn't paid the next install-ment of your ground rent? You don't end up leaning against the wall in the mummy museum in Guanajuato?"

"No." She shook her head firmly.

"Has the twenty-four hour law changed?"

"No, it's still on the books. The difference is that there are more options now. Action is still taken in a mat-ter of hours. The body has to be available twelve hours before anything can be done to it, because there have been instances in history where people have been buried alive."

"An Edgar Allen Poe situation," I said. "You end up scratching on the lid of your coffin from inside."

Natalie Hardy nodded. "After that, it has to be taken care of as soon as possible. If you are cremated, that's done within twenty-four hours. The same is true if you are embalmed. But then, whatever other arrange-ment you make, a funeral or a memorial service, it's han-dled in whatever other time period you choose."

"Within reason."

"Yes, always within reason."

"So once you're embalmed, if that is what you

wish, your heirs could then go beyond that twenty-four hour period and make other arrangements. That's the new flexibility. How does a person go about setting up a relationship with the Association?"

"To become a member, we are now computerized and we have a twenty-four hour cell phone available. The executive secretary handles everything that comes up for a member's needs. You connect with her and fill out an application. You can go into all kinds of things, like where your will and other documents are kept. Basically we're here to connect with your friends or family, anyone who would be taking care of your affairs on the other end."

"What happens if I'm sixty years old and I think this is a great concept so I pay my $1,000 to set it up and then I live another twenty-five years. Does the cost go up then, and if so do you come back to me for more money?"

She shook her head. "No, and this is interesting. As I said, we give people their money back if their plans change, and we have never asked for an increase for the current costs. For example, I've been a member now for sixteen years, and the cost has more than doubled. Because I paid what I did then, nothing more is asked of me. If for some reason we find that the costs are greatly increasing, we might have to change our practice, and ask for more, but we never have to date, and we don't plan to now. The other thing is that when we get the one-time payment, it's invested safely so that there is income to pay the salaries of the two staff members. Those two are also board members. One is the executive secretary and the other is treasurer."

"How many members are there now?"

"Over four hundred."

"I want to ask you one more thing. What would you say to people who are settling into San Miguel, enjoying the expat atmosphere and expecting to stay and live out the rest of their years here. What would you tell them about the Association?"

"From first hand experience I can say it's an enormous gift for you to give to those who will be dealing with your affairs after your passing. I know it takes a huge weight off my mind, because I don't feel like I'm leaving any other business behind."

"So there's not going to be someone in Cleveland who has to deal with this from 2,000 miles away on no notice. To start paying your cremation or funeral home bills out of their own pocket as your estate gets processed. That could take months or years, if you have property down here."

"Exactly. We have had situations where it's enormously awkward for people to get down here without any notice. They're often younger, they're working and with a family, or they may be distant relatives because there is no immediate family. Setting this up is a great gift. From my perspective, it's probably the best one you can give. There's one more aspect of this, and it's an important one. The Twenty-four Hour Association is the only organization here that can register the death of a person without having the next of kin present. The executive secretary has special legal dispensation to do this. This fact separates us from any other prepaid plan in San Miguel. It is very important when you think of the alternative, and someone needing to travel down here from elsewhere on short notice."

I was still thinking about Natalie Hardy's last comment as I said goodbye and walked slowly down the stairs to the street. At the end she had hit directly on the most critical point. It was not only a great gift to the person who would have to wrap up the details of your life. Even if they knew what to do, how could they get down here to do it within such a short time frame? What if they didn't have a current passport? Naturally, the Mexican laws were not made with expats in mind.

Here is the contact information for the Association:

Executive Secretary: Linda Cooper home, 415 185 2023 (add 011 52 if calling from the US or Canada). Email: linkaycooper@yahoo.com or sec@24assoc.com

Website: www.24assoc.com

Several times during that night I awakened thinking about the Twenty-four Hour Association. It made so much sense. The following morning I headed for the Panteón at about nine o'clock. I hadn't been there for more than a year; the last time was probably on the occasion of the Day of the Dead, when all the graves are decorated. Now I wanted to see it again without the crowd. Many of the past actors in this expat drama were there, at least the ones who had stayed for their final curtain call, and I felt I had gained some insight into those end-of-days stories. Since it's a place of such unique atmosphere, I had even once placed an important scene at the Panteón in one of my mysteries, the one titled *The Jericho Journals*.

On leaving her house, I had asked Natalie if she understood why the expats felt they needed a separate burial ground in the 1970s. Her feeling was that it may have been no more than a desire for a different style or design of their grave markers. Combined with a timely offer from the city of San Miguel de Allende, the idea may have seemed irresistible. I was not tempted to see any segregationist motive in it. After all, these were all people who had chosen to live among Mexicans, so what was wrong with being buried among them?

Entering from a quiet street behind the thoroughfare called Salida a Celaya, the principal and primarily Mexican section of the cemetery is a riot of form and color. Most of the graves are surface burials. It is as if death is the moment to break loose and shine, especially if you'd had little chance to do it in your working life. Many of the inscriptions address God directly. Relatives scrawl their messages to the deceased. The burials are crowded together elbow to elbow, and I wondered if this doesn't express in some way the Mexican view of personal space, because here people come much closer when they talk to each other. Expats are often disconcerted by it. Maybe that more intimate sense of distance continues after death.

In this large densely packed space, tomb architecture is a folk art and a vivid sense of spiritual improvisation is its muse. Some elements, like columns, arched windows, and wrought iron enclosures are traditional and familiar. Others come straight out of the family's vibrant dreams, conforming to nothing so much as grief and celebration combined. At the back, a long row of stacked niches offers a more restrained presentation, often with the concrete framed within the square opening covered with emotional fingertip messages scrawled in the mortar while still wet.

There is no doubt that this reflects a different view of life as well as of death. The people I saw around me were not gone, they had simply moved out of their houses into a more communal residence. But they were still accessible if you needed to talk to them, and they didn't mind some company. Bring along a liter bottle of beer and share it.

In a back corner I found the iron gates that opened through a tall, sculpted hedge into the expat section. As I entered they swung shut behind me. Immediately I encountered a different atmosphere inside. Smaller, of course, this enclosed plot is paved with uniform low maintenance gravel and divided by red brick pathways. Cool shade trees abound, a mix of palms, cypress, long needle pine, and mesquite. When I paused, directly across from me was the grave of Marie Van Horn Charlton from 1987, the widow of Rear Admiral Alex Charlton, who had organized the Twenty-four Hour Association.

In the shady branches overhead the mourning doves mewed softly. The only other sound came from the groundskeepers in the main section far beyond the hedge. Two of them were using machetes to chop out the grass that came up between the paving stones on the paths.

Most of the expat grave markers are designed as a plain, arched, buff-colored limestone, although some were different. Usually they were fronted by a patch of ivy. The older ones can often be a flat layer of brick with a square of engraved stone in the center (1970s). To the left of the entry and further down I found the fanciful grave marker of Toller Cranston, the Canadian Olympic skater. *Toller Artist*, it reads, flagging his interest in

painting, but with no mention of his last name. The epi-
taph reads, *Zero Tollerance*. (sic) He died at the beginning
of 2015, at the age of sixty-five.

Along the back wall the rows of niches are all
framed in red stucco. Many are divided into four com-
partments for cremated remains. There are plenty of
open spaces available for the rest of us. All around me
are the people who made the American and Canadian
community of San Miguel what it is today. They rest
here comfortably as if at home. I use that word advisedly
in the sense of a place where one would wish to come to
earth at the end, at rest among friends.

This place possesses its own calm texture and
mood, and if it reflects a different view of death, then
it also does of life. Although some have crosses or a Star
of David, none of these stones cries out to God or Jesus. Visitors are mainly shown the dates of passage, of
coming and going, with an occasional family sentiment.
That is all. The dead are restrained in their presentation
here, as if it is a calmer and more defined way to be. The
graves are farther apart; they give these silent residents
more elbowroom for an eternity that is not so densely
subdivided.

Here the expats are more formal in death than
their Mexican neighbors. Once the end overtakes them,
their submission is quieter, and no one holds raucous parties for them on the Day of the Dead in early November.

On those long fiesta nights, they may turn over in their lengthy sleep, wishing that those on the other side of the hedge would soon finish their revels and that their relatives would go back home. As in life, even in death our Mexican neighbors still tend to party longer and harder than we do.

PART TWO

PEOPLE

CHAPTER TEN
THE AUSTINS

It will be no surprise that my visit to the Panteón put me in the mood to connect with some living residents, and I had earlier arranged a conversation with a couple who had been here long enough to settle in and develop some perspective, but for a short enough time to be still discovering new things. Neither newbies nor old hands, was the way I thought of them.

Even more, I found myself ready to write about some individuals who had made the leap. How did the reality mesh with their dream? Had they done enough homework to avoid having every day begin with a surprise? How much resilience do you need to make it here? Sometimes "how to do it" is better illustrated by "what did you do and how did it go?" I headed up to one of the hillsides overlooking town.

El Paraiso is a relatively recent gated community at the top of the slope of the Querétaro Road where it levels off not far from the Luciérnaga shopping mall. As in the older parts of town, the houses are built shoulder to shoulder with open spaces within the walls to furnish privacy and terraces overhead to capture the views. Most expats tend to prefer the traditional style of Mexican house construction, using columns, arches, and an interior courtyard with a fountain and garden. Mexicans who are purchasing homes in this bracket typically do not. They want to be what they think of as cutting edge. However, I find Mexican modern design to often be aggressively sterile, and almost abstract in feeling. It offers little warmth, and appears more conceptual than livable.

The El Paraiso neighborhood (which means paradise) style is not predictably either. Within a wide variety of configurations it offers a range of exterior design concepts I would mostly call soft contemporary. The surface textures are richer and more inviting than Mexican modern, even if they don't use a great deal of embellishment. I have been told by other residents there that the interiors can reflect nearly anything from traditional colonial to Moroccan to bare-bones minimalist. Viewed from an upper terrace, this community offers the feel of a real place, even if recent in its origin. It seems friendly and it's walkable.

Until the day of the conversation I was headed for, I had not met Larry and Jo Austin, and I was running late. Coming up the Salida a Querétaro I found that an accident had blocked two of the four lanes and traffic was crawling. Once through the gate after this delay, the street signage was minimal and I had only the house numbers to go on. When I pulled up and rang the doorbell I was twenty minutes late. Mexicans are more relaxed about being on time, and I've gotten that way with them too, but dealing with expats brings out the more rigid gringo time sense in me.

Jo Austin opened the door to my apology and brought me inside.

Thinking of home, this was where Larry and Jo Austin had chosen to come to earth in San Miguel. From the exterior, their house was typical of the neighborhood, and walking in I didn't feel like I had entered some architect's minimal idea of a house. They have done some serious remodeling on the main floor that made it livable and inviting.

We settled in the kitchen at the corner of a long counter where the voice recorder could take in the three of us. Both the Austins are trim and outgoing people. Larry is more gray, with short hair and a half-inch beard. I already knew a handful of facts about them, information that had helped me assemble the questions, and I had furnished them with the question list ahead of time so they could discuss the answers. I always feel I can get a more thoughtful conversation that way, since they are never taken by surprise.

"Let's start with some background about what you did in your past life and how you came to settle in San Miguel."

Larry began. "I was a federal employee, an air traffic controller. I took an early retirement because of health issues in the 1990s, so I've actually been retired longer than I worked. I became a househusband for Jo. I'm originally from Alabama, and I entered the service in Texas and stayed there in Texas for my whole career."

"I was born and raised in Oklahoma," Jo said. "I moved to Texas in 1973. There I met Larry, and I was the finance director for an automobile dealership for twenty-eight years. Larry was a great househusband."

"Was that the kind of business where you were arranging auto loans and approving or rejecting people for credit?"

"Yes."

"Then at some point as you were considering retirement, you found out about San Miguel and thought, well, maybe we'd like to live in México and not stay in the States anymore."

"Right," Larry said. "In 2005 we came down here for six months. What led to that was that in 2001 we were both diagnosed with cancer. We went through chemo together, and luckily we both came out on the other side OK. After that experience we decided that maybe a change would be in order."

"I can easily see that. You had nothing to lose then. I would think of it as a 'take charge' moment."

"Right, and we had gotten a little tired of a

car-centric society, where you needed a car to go anywhere, so we started to investigate places that might offer a different culture, yet be close enough to get back to the States if we needed to for health reasons. México was the obvious choice, since Canada was too cold. At that time, AARP did an article about three places to retire in México, and one of them was San Miguel. We didn't like the other two; I think they were beach places. We didn't care that much for the beach, so we came here for six months in 2005. Our original plan was to spend six months each in areas where we thought we might like to settle. But by the time the six months here were up, our next destination, which was Dolphin Island, Alabama, where we had already rented a house for six months, Katrina had come along and wiped that house out."

"We didn't have a house to go to anymore," Jo added with a shrug.

"Did that halt your search for a place to settle?"

"Well, then we went back to Texas and Jo's old company contacted her and wanted her to come back to work. So she did and we stayed for eleven more years. The climate was still difficult, and politically we were a lot further to the left than the vast majority of our neighbors. And after the 2008 election, the gap between people got more dramatic, and the hostility was growing against anyone that didn't follow the Texas line. So we were tired of August being 115° and January being zero, and we were sitting around one day and Jo said, 'You know, Larry, if something happened to you, I'd have very few friends here, and really not much social life at all.'"

Jo was nodding. "That's right, except for our good friends across the street. They were like-minded. We had traveled with them and they were our best friends."

"Would it be fair to say that the political culture there had a lot to do with your comfort level?" I already knew that the great majority of expats in San Miguel would identify themselves as liberals, even if not strictly as Democratic Party members, although quite often they did.

"Yes," Jo said, "because we did not talk politics with anybody except our close friends. People can get ugly."

"So your close friends there would've tended to be only people who felt as you did?"

"Yes."

"Our next-door neighbor was a good guy and a good neighbor," Larry said, "and we talked politics one time. Before he spun around and walked off, his last comment to me was, 'You go ahead then and vote for Sambo, and I'll cancel you out.' That was the kind of environment that we lived in." He relaxed back into his chair and covered his face for a moment. I was thinking about one of the first books I'd had as a kid. *Little Black Sambo*, where a tiger had chased the children around a tree and they somehow turned into butter, but in my recollection the black children were from India. But anyway.

"So for me," Larry said, "it was more about the climate, between the winter and the summer. We lived in a golf community and we tried to play golf, but it was so hot we really couldn't get out and play in the summertime."

"And what part of Texas was this?"

"Fort Worth."

"So you came down here again in 2016, is that right?"

"We sold our home and came here on April 12 and rented a house three streets down while we looked for a house to buy," Jo said. "We found this one and closed on it three weeks later."

"What do you think now about this El Paraiso neighborhood?"

"I love it."

"So do I."

"What is it about this area?"

"It's mainly the people here," Larry said. "San Miguel in general, for sure, but El Paraíso in particular. When we were in the rental, the woman who owned it lived across the street from us, and on the second or third day we were there she had a party for us. She invited all the neighbors over and we got to meet people. Yesterday we went to an art function. This evening we're going to a party down the street. Tomorrow we're going to a party in *colonia* (neighborhood) Independencia with all the people we have met here. Life in this town is amazing."

"So you would characterize that by saying social acceptance here comes with a certain ease, a kind of fluidity that you might not have encountered in other places where you've lived in the past?"

"Yes, we have not seen it like this elsewhere, and this may sound silly, but one of the reasons for that I think is the sidewalks, because I believe that sidewalks make for neighborhoods. In the States we had never lived in a neighborhood with sidewalks before. When you wanted to walk somewhere you had to walk in the street."

"And the people are so friendly here," Jo added. "When I get on the bus everybody smiles and speaks to me, and I'm talking about the Mexicans as well as the gringos. They are really nice people."

Part of it too, I was thinking, is that as expats we are all living here in a special status, almost conditional, and that tends to throw us together psychologically. "Nearly two years after your arrival, do you look at moving to México as a journey toward something or away from something? Might it have been an escape?"

"It has been sort of both," Jo said, "and I think's it's been an exciting journey at this stage of our lives, getting out and meeting new people in a new culture. We don't speak the language much yet, but we're picking it up slowly but surely. I think it's a journey towards something."

Larry was nodding as she finished. "It's both for me. I was raised on the move, every three or four years. Living that way is kind of in my DNA. Sometimes I get itchy feet after a few years. Texas had worn thin for me, especially with my heart disease. You can't get outside sometimes, you can't do anything. Coming here, it's a different culture where people look you in the eye when you're walking down the street. They smile. It's such a different environment than the United States."

Jo raised both her hands for emphasis. "And walking here has been so healthy for him. He's lost over fifty pounds. We've been eating all sorts of fresh fruits and vegetables from the Tuesday Market."

"That's a wonderful place. I have a segment on it in this book. It's easy to be locavores here. Did you keep your U.S. healthcare insurance? That is a dilemma for a lot of people, since you cannot use Medicare here."

"We are very fortunate," Larry said. "We're both on Medicare, we kept that, but being a retired federal employee I also kept my federal insurance. In the States it acts as a supplement to Medicare. Here it acts as primary coverage. We just scan our receipts and email them back to them. Then they send us a check. We are very fortunate to have that."

I asked about their ages, and Jo confessed to

being sixty-five, and Larry, seventy-one. Throughout the conversation so far I had heard no sound at all from outside. From the busy Salida a Querétaro, about two blocks away, nothing had reached us at all.

"When you were still back in Texas, was there a single thing, or was it a gradual trend or drift that led you to move down here?"

"For me," Larry said, "it was a gradual trend that started—I could tolerate the weather because I could stay in the house—but it started after the 2008 election with the Tea Party movement. I grew up in Alabama, so I know racism intimately. I know all of its forms no matter where they come from. This was just pure, absolute racism. It was really upsetting. I could not believe that America was turning a corner and heading back. And then with the climate as well, I was just wanting something different."

"And you, Jo?"

"I feel that way too. It was about having something different."

"But this has to be a huge change to adapt to, even if that was exactly what you felt you wanted. At the age you are does it take a special kind of attitude to be so accepting of change?"

Jo nodded vigorously. "I think it does."

"It takes a degree of curiosity," Larry said. "We can't be so certain of what we know. You have to be ready to find out there are things you don't know."

"Are you also ready then to be wrong?"

"Sure."

"Maybe," Jo said.

"One thing that keeps me going as a writer is that I have to always be ready to fall down. To try something that doesn't work and still get up again and work to get it right. It's all about taking chances."

"I understand that," Jo said.

"But I don't think everyone in the third act of their lives has retained that ability," I said. "Life itself gets chancier as you age and for some people arriving at certainty becomes more important, even if that's often illusory."

"No," Larry added, "there's a lot of arrogance of certainty. I struggle with that too. I think it was Gandhi that said a friendship that requires agreement on all things is not worthy of the term. I like to be contrary with others and have disagreements, but without being disagreeable. A cliché perhaps, but I enjoy people who think differently than I do. We can always learn from each other."

"Now, after being here for approximately a year and a half of settling in, have you discovered what you miss about the States?"

"Well, that would be shopping," Jo said with little hesitation. "Being able to find here different products in the grocery store that we otherwise have to smuggle back when we come across the border. That's my big thing that I miss, and friends and family. That's it."

"Well, what I miss most about the States is the familiarity with the language. Being able to walk into a store and being able to converse freely and openly and understand what is said back to you."

"Does your family come down?"

"Yes." Both of them answered at once.

"Do they find it strange that you moved to México? That's hard for some people to accept."

Larry responded. "Our youngest son lives in Austin and he works in the tech industry. He did not want to come down here last March. His wife said, 'yes we are going to take the kids and we are going to visit your mom and dad.' And he did, but he was still trying to come up with an excuse not to on the way to the airport. Like he had to go back home, he couldn't go right then. But once he got here, he loved it. He can't wait to come back. He was just afraid, afraid the cartels were going to hold them up on the way here from the airport."

"Was that his first trip?"

"Yes," Jo said.

"What would you change about San Miguel?"

"When we looked at your questions," Jo said, "Larry and I both said the traffic. The traffic is horrendous here. We don't go into *el centro* now on weekends because it's so busy. But when we opened *Atención* today (the bilingual weekly newspaper for San Miguel) and the front-page article is all about parking meters, and how you're going to have to park outside. I think that's wonderful. *El centro* should be more for pedestrians, they should block off more streets."

This plan was ultimately dropped, although other options are being considered.

"I worry that San Miguel is becoming a bubble," Larry said, "what with real estate and tourism. There's been so much press in the last year or year and a half about how it's the best small city in the world. You have to wonder whether it's a bubble that's going to burst."

Jo nodded. "You know, houses in this neighborhood are selling almost as fast as they go on the market now, and for prices way above what we were looking at only a year and a half ago. I think it's all because of the good press."

"And this neighborhood is selling today mainly in the three and four hundred thousand dollar range?" I said.

"Yes."

"The next question, and we may have dealt with some of this already, is how the U.S. has changed between 2005 and your departure in 2016."

"It's now a lot more divided into an us and them attitude. Here, we don't understand the local politics. It's not a concern to us," Larry said.

"Is that a relief?"

"Yes, it's a big relief."

"Is that true for you too, Jo?"

"I think so, yes."

"One thing I've been exploring in this book is people's idea of home. Even as you settle in here, is the U.S. still your home in a larger sense? If it is, what would or will it take to make México home?"

They were both silent for a moment, but Jo spoke first. "It's home because that's where we were raised and that's where our friends and family are. But now when we go to Texas for doctors or whatever, we cannot wait to come 'home' to our house here in México."

"So at least there's an ambivalent edge to the idea of 'home.' Emotionally, what does that mean when you say, I want to go home? What images come into your mind when you think that coming home means coming back to México?"

"It's the people around us, it's our community now. That's how I feel it most," Jo said.

"And it's how little risk we feel. We did a lot of work with this house and we love it. It fits us perfectly. Of course, there are still neighbors and friends that we miss. But you can go to the Tuesday Market or *el centro*, and I love going to *el centro* and just walking around. I think it's one of the most incredible places in the world. And we've been everywhere from Bali to Europe, to South America, everywhere. This place is really unique."

"The question I have here next is whether home might be no more than where you are at any moment, but it's obviously more than that from what you've said. It's not just in your head, it's your social connections..."

"The physical presence of our stuff," Larry said. "We brought our stuff with us."

"We spent a ton of money bringing all of our stuff."

"We've been married thirty-eight years," Larry said. "There are so many things we've accumulated, and having that, well that to us is home. You could put that stuff in any building anywhere and that would be home."

"When we stayed here in 2005 we rented a furnished house. One of the things I missed most then was that we didn't have our things. We had our clothes and that was it. I wanted my stuff. Does that make sense?"

"Yes. There is a chapter in this book called Death and Dying. I don't know if you've visited the Panteón here. It's the more recent one, the in town cemetery."

"Down by the Ancha de San Antonio?" Jo said. I nodded. "I went there for Day of the Dead."

"And did you see the expat section?"

Both answered together. "Yes."

"Here's a hard question. Let me ask if you plan to die here."

"Yes, but we'll be cremated."

Larry's face took on a more thoughtful look. "And that was one of the reasons... We end to analyze things, and one of the reasons we moved here was for our end of life experience. We have more yesterdays than tomorrows now. By the time the federal government offered its employees and retirees long-term care, I'd already had heart disease and cancer, and Jo had already had cancer. We weren't eligible for it. As we age we don't want to burden our children, for our sake and theirs. This is such a more caring environment, and an easier way to end your life. You don't have to go bankrupt to die here."

This was as good a way of saying it as I've ever heard, but I didn't interrupt him.

"There are affordable people who will come to your home and take care of you. There are doctors that will come in and hook you up and as they're going out will say, 'And don't hit that button more than ten times.'"

We all recognized the subtext in this statement. I looked at him for a long moment. "I think you have recognized a very important truth about this place. Whatever else it might be, it's humane."

"Yes." We all looked at the table for a moment.

"To move on from that thought, what have you learned by living in México that you couldn't have learned by staying in the States?"

"The culture, you know," Jo said, "like Day of the

Dead. I'd heard of Day of the Dead all my life in Texas, but I didn't realize what it entailed. It is beautiful. I love going to the cemetery." She gave me a grim smile.

"Since we've been here, we've gone to Mexico City twice, we've been to Puebla, Guanajuato, and we've been to the butterfly sanctuary in Michoacán. Those are places that are so different. I mean, there are some great places in the United States, wonderful places, like the national parks. But here, there's the great variety in the culture, and the cities; Mexico City is one of our favorite cities in the world. The museums, and the Polanco district is a lot like Paris. And Guanajuato is a beautiful city, it's incredible."

"The tunnels in Guanajuato are scary," Jo said.

That city, which is our state capital, is honeycombed with tunnels that were originally designed to divert floodwaters away from the local mines in the rainy season. That part of the state is rich in silver, and the largest silver mine in the world, the Valenciana, is on the western edge of the city.

"Before we started this conversation I told you I always write a book, any book, with a particular target reader in mind. In this case it's a person who is wondering whether the kind of experience that you've had in moving here and settling in would be a good fit for him or her. Knowing what you know now, and having the entire experience of moving here still fresh in your mind, what would you say to that person today?"

"Do your research and come down for a visit," Jo said in a firm tone. "Try it out first for a few months, and if it is really for you, then make the move."

"I think I would say pretty much the same thing. I think you need to come and rent something that is going to be equivalent to what you plan to live in. It's easy to come here and splurge a bit and rent a home that would cost you two million dollars to buy, when you've only got a five hundred thousand dollar budget. Rent something appropriate, learn the neighborhoods, get out and meet the people. Walk the streets, talk to people in the *jardín* (our main square). Plan to stay three or four months and realize there are going to be good days and bad days."

"Yes," Jo added, "because when we first moved into this house, we thought, oh no! That was because we ended up renovating this whole bottom floor. It was a mess. There were many nights when we almost cried ourselves to sleep, thinking what have we done? In some ways this house was awful, but we wanted to be in this neighborhood and there wasn't much to choose from when we were looking."

"So spend the time," Larry said, nodding slowly for emphasis, "do the research, and by all means don't listen to your friends in the States. Don't judge México if you've only been to Cancún or Puerto Vallarta. That's like going to Las Vegas and thinking you've been to the

United States. This is a totally unique and different environment."

That seemed to sum it up. I gathered my equipment and shook hands all around.

Talking with the Austins had been an enjoyable conversation. I liked their frankness and I came away feeling they had batted the questions around between themselves before they met with me. I also always prefer talking to a couple when that's possible, because the differences in their answers can be revealing. The interview had taken place at a time when they were no longer newbies, nor were they yet old México hands either. Enough time had passed to give them perspective on their experience, but they were still fresh enough to recall their arrival and settling in.

As I got into the car I also realized I'd had an insight myself. It was that death is also part of the question of where home might be. Planning to finish your life here is literally a way of coming to earth, and it is to be fundamentally home in the broadest sense. Most people would not want to die in a strange land, and in planning to end their lives in México, the Austins had clearly made their choice of where their final home would be. It its way, that is the deepest of commitments.

CHAPTER ELEVEN
JENNY McCARTHY ROMO
&
PRO MUSICA

The music scene in San Miguel is one of many venues that provide endless opportunities for entertainment and enlightenment. Among them one great resource is Pro Musica. It presents a program of classical concerts beginning in the fall of each year. In addition to individual event tickets, supporting memberships are available at progressive levels. They carry benefits like preferential seating and invitations to cocktail parties to meet the artists. It's a congenial group, and my wife and I have been patrons for several years now. The person we always deal with on memberships and reservations is a young woman named Jenny Mc-Carthy Romo. From dealing with her over a number of seasons, I knew she has a strong business head combined with a relaxed and friendly manner. She's a natural to front the day-to-day operations for Pro Musica.

From the perspective of a person who was not party to the inner workings of the organization, Jenny seemed to me to be the ultimate insider. She was the one with her hands on the levers and the gears of Pro Musica. While I already knew that she did not select the artists for the concerts, she also told me that she has an associate who handles the lodging for the performers, their airport transit, and their other personal needs. Their hosts are often the every day contact people for their visits. Jenny is more the member person, the public face for people who join and support the Pro Musica programs.

We met for a conversation late on a Monday morning in the middle of May at St. Paul's Episcopal Church. This is the venerable hall where the concerts are held. It's on Calle Cardo half a block from the intersection with the Ancha de San Antonio. With good acoustics and an interior that is easily reconfigured for chamber ensembles or solo artists, it would be difficult to name a better concert venue, at least on this scale. We needed a quiet place to record this conversation, since Jenny's home, where she works in the absence of a formal office, also includes five dogs, two cats, and a two-year-old child, and that's assuming her older child is in school. That's too much potential chaos for my delicately calibrated voice recorder, which does not easily distinguish between a recital of Enrico Caruso and a catfight.

Jenny was waiting for me inside and for our conversation we chose the conference room, with doors open to the outside along the back.

Jenny McCarthy Romo is a tall, attractive woman with dark hair nearly reaching her shoulders. When I offered to put down thirty as her age in this chapter, she outbid me at thirty-six. I always try to lose contests like that and I rarely fail. She was wearing pale jeans and a yellow sleeveless top with a scooped neck. It was going to be a warm day for a relaxed conversation. May is usually the warmest month here.

Aside from exploring her position at Pro Musica as both a major cultural resource and an educational charity for local students, I wanted her contribution to these conversations because of her youth in a community that is both driven by, and the beneficiary of, people of retirement age. I needed the fresh and atypical perspective of a young expat, one whose roots here had developed in a somewhat different manner from most others.

I placed her at the head of the conference table; after all this was her turf. We started with some idle chatter, which led to the idea that I was going to ask her to sign the usual release allowing me to quote her for this book. Then we began.

"I have to say I'm delighted to find a younger person like you living here as an expat, working and raising a family. Can we start by you telling me how you learned about San Miguel and came down here?"

As with the Austins, she had seen these questions before, since I wanted her to have time to consider any that seemed to require some thought.

"I was eleven years old when my mom decided we were going to start traveling to México for spring break. The first year we went to Acapulco. Even back then it was kind of dirty and seedy, and my mom loved it. The next year, when I was twelve, I said, 'Where are we going this year?' She had seen an article in the travel section of the New York Times, on the front page, about San Miguel de Allende. She had heard of San Miguel because we were from a little town in Pennsylvania called New Hope, and it's an artist colony. In the seventies a lot of the artists from New Hope were coming down for classes here at the Instituto Allende. She said, 'We're going to San Miguel!' My dad had no idea where the place was. We got here and it was March, the dry season. I had never seen a desert in my life. The drive in from León has never seemed attractive to me, even now. My dad and I were freaking out about where my mother had taken us. I was thinking it would all be dust and donkeys, but we pulled into San Miguel and every criticism I could think of ended right there. That was in 1994. This town was really different then." Her eyebrows went up and she looked out the back windows for a long moment. "It was quiet and sleepy and colonial and artistic. It was amazing. We fell in love right away. My mom asked me on that trip whether I might want to move down here to learn Spanish."

"And you were twelve years old."

"Yes, and I said, 'Sure, let's do it.' I was at that age when I wasn't nervous about anything. You get to an age later when the world starts imposing its expectations on you. It never occurred to me that it meant moving to another country. So we vacationed here one more time and then in 1996 my mom and I moved here in August. My dad worked in New York, so he would come down once a month for a week."

"You were fourteen then."

"Right, so we spent a year and a half here. I went to a local school, José Vasconselos. I wanted to stay but after that year I was going to be a sophomore in high school and I started to get concerned about taking SATs and ACTs, and applying for college. When I went back they accepted my year and a half here and I finished high school there. That's how I ended up here."

"Then did you come back here right after high school?"

"No, first I went to college in Memphis, Tennessee. After college I was hired by Pfizer Pharmaceuticals as a sales rep."

"Was chemistry your major? Pharmacy?"

"No, it was political science, with a minor in history. I wanted to be a lawyer, but my dad very rightly told me, 'You think with your heart, not your brain. You would not like being a lawyer, but if you want to try it, let's go for it. I'll pay for law school, and I will support you in your decision.'"

"But you didn't study law." This made me think of many other dads who would never have been so supportive. How fortunate Jenny had been to still have choices then.

"No, I took his advice, so I was hired by Pfizer with a background having nothing to do with their business, and they moved me up to Cape Cod. I only lasted two years. I had a beautiful house on the water, I was making lots of money, and I was miserable. I didn't know anybody. I was a townie and I didn't meet anybody. In that job, you don't work in an office; you work out of your car. Everybody there in the winter is old."

"That sounds a little bit like San Miguel," I said. She let this pass.

"I hated it, and I only stayed on partly because my dad was really proud of me. Finally I got up the nerve to tell him I was miserable, and then I sold everything and I came down here because I didn't know what else I wanted to do."

"How did that feel?"

"Well, as I said, I already had a history with this place. My sister had moved down here. She's sixteen years older than I am, so she's more like an aunt. This is actually the first time we've ever lived close to each other."

"And she's here now?"

"Yes. One of my best friends was going to school in Puebla, but her roots were here in San Miguel. My mother had passed away and we had a house here. My dad was in the process of selling it. I said, 'Wait six months, wait until I have a job.' It just seemed like the right thing to do. I was running away and the idea of moving home at twenty-three would've made me feel like a complete failure. My dad said, 'I'll get you a job, and we'll see where you want to live.'

"I said that New York was not my thing either. So I came down here."

"And you got married."

"I met my husband five days after I got here."

"Is he in politics?"

"He is."

"As a career?"

"Well, he's a lawyer. He's head of the Green Party here and this is the third campaign we've gone through. The first time they won and the second time they did not and we're hoping now for another win in July. He's going for a city council seat."

"Please tell me a little more about your family. What's it like raising kids in this kind of environment? Do they find friends here easily?"

"They do. They were born here in San Miguel. My daughter is two and a half and my son is seven and a half. They are five years apart almost to the day. I love living here. I have a group of American friends that I've just gotten to know in the past couple of years. My husband is Mexican and my family is Mexican. All my friends were Mexican. I really didn't have anything to do with the American community here of any age, and just in the past two years this group has come together."

"That must be rewarding."

"I didn't live any of my adulthood in the United States. I moved away when I was twenty-two. I had been paying my own bills, but I don't really know how things work in the States. I don't know what it's like to have children there, or what it's like to have a relationship and a marriage there. For all intents and purposes, I'm a Mexican."

"Do you still try to preserve some of the American childhood traditions for your kids?"

"Yes, we do. My husband is half American. His mother was from Wisconsin, so most of the traditions that we have are American. We also celebrate all the Mexican holidays. We celebrate Three Kings Day (January 6, the day when holiday gifts are distributed). We party hard in September when my kids' birthdays are, along with Mexican Independence Day. The friends that I've made who are American say something that I feel just from living here. I can give my children a lifestyle in San Miguel that is very hard to find in the U.S. I don't have to work twenty-four hours a day. I'm lucky to have a job that allows me all the time I wish with my kids. I've had a maid at home who's helped me for the last eight years. I have my freedom, which gives them freedom. My kids play outside every day and they grow up here more like we did in the eighties before everyone got freaked out about kids being kidnapped. Now the helicopter parents watch what they eat and what they do."

"Do you feel the school resources are adequate for them?"

"They will be. The school my son goes to is amazing. The standards are just as high was he would get in the United States. But San Miguel does not at this point have a high school that I would send him to." She continued to talk about several options in the neighboring cities of Querétaro and Celaya, each about an hour's commute away.

"But you are some distance off from having to deal with that."

"I am." Her expression suggested she planned to be ready for it when it came.

"What are your longer-term plans? Do you see yourself as a permanent resident? You've already mentioned that you have a sister here. Do you have any other family in town? Does San Miguel feel like a real home to you?"

Jenny went on to describe her in-laws. "I don't see

myself going anywhere else. This is home. Sometimes I'll get an urge to move back to the States and see what it's like there. I think that's a dream that would turn out not to be the way I think of it. Of course this is home for my husband, above all. I wouldn't try to force him to do something on a whim."

"It doesn't sound like it's much of a sacrifice to stay here."

"No. My husband works, but he's also at every single school recital, and all the other occasions and events."

"Do you find yourself comparing México with the U.S.?"

"All the time! My friends and I have a joke about the 875,000th thing we hate about living here. But we'd have the same jokes about living in the States. It wouldn't be any less."

"My mantra for living here is 'Stop Making Sense.'"

"Exactly. Most things I love about México, but there are some things I can't stand about it. If I were in this same place in my life in the States there would be tons of things I'd be complaining about there too."

"It's not about finding perfection," I said. "It never was and it never could be. How did you come to be connected with Pro Musica? What is your position, if you can define it?"

"The word that describes it best is general manager. I run the show in terms of the details. Michael Pearl, the founder and president, chooses the artists, signs the contracts, and fluffs up the feathers of a lot of our donors. I try to do everything else. The way I found out about Pro Musica is kind of funny. I had been working here for the same family my husband worked for. They owned a cable company and some bars and restaurants. I was managing their hotel and it was becoming too much for me. My son was a year and a half old and the boss needed me to spend more and more time in the hotel. I quit one morning and that afternoon I went to have coffee with a friend and I told her I needed a job."

By an indirect route, that friend connected her with Pro Musica. "This was in August of 2012. I met with Michael Pearl on September eighteenth and started work on September nineteenth."

"I don't want to make you try to be the spokesperson for Pro Musica, but what is their mission as you see it day to day?"

"That's a good point. What people see on the outside is an important concert series. What they don't always see behind that is that our larger job as an organization is to bring music to children and adolescents. It started out by just giving music classes to one or two schools in the campo. Now we give classes to more than 900 kids. We have a music academy, a children's orchestra, and a youth orchestra that had been failing while under control of the *municipio* and is now flourishing with Pro Musica." (The San Miguel de Allende *municipio* is an entity larger than just the city, and somewhat similar to a county in the U.S.)

"In addition to this, how many regular concerts do you give in a season?"

"Between twenty-five and thirty. That includes the gala, the opera and some benefit performances. Some people say, well you're giving them music classes when these kids need housing and food, but if you look at the plan and the outline you'll see it's not just teaching them music. They're taught how to stand up in front of their peers, how to have more confidence in themselves. They're taught geography and history. Tim Hazell, the head of our education outreach, teaches them a new way to look at the world."

This got me going. "Well, tell me if I'm wrong, but I've been talking to other people working with NGOs for this book, and it sounds to me like the music teaching program dovetails very well indeed with the whole spectrum of the other programs. Not every organization has to be furnishing meals or housing or health care, not that they aren't critical, but this is part of a much larger effort, and you are offering a program that touches their soul. As a painter and a writer, I think that's essential in any person's upbringing. Art is the first thing to disappear when you're very poor, even though it's the most uplifting part of life. Do you have a background in music yourself?"

"No. I took guitar in fifth grade."

"What parts of Pro Musica do you enjoy the most?"

"Most probably it would be dealing with the members. It's my face they see at all the concerts. I've been here for six years and I know everybody. With a lot of them I know when they've been sick, I know their grandkids' names; I know where they go when they're not here. I never would've had a chance to meet a group of people like I've met through Pro Musica.

"Beyond the members, I would have to add that I truly love working with Michael Pearl as well. It is definitely a highlight. Not everyone can say that their boss treats them as an equal, but I can. I am lucky to have such a great relationship with him."

"How do the performing artists find lodging here? Do local people put them up?" I was thinking of the New York star violinist appearing for breakfast in his pajamas looking for kosher potato pancakes.

"Yes, they do. Our housing coordinator finds lodging for the artists coming in. In all my time, we've only had one artist who was flabbergasted at the idea that we would put him in somebody's home, someone he didn't know. The others have all loved it here and are fine with the idea of staying in a private home. One artist said to me, 'Oftentimes I go to cities where I end up sitting by myself at Denny's in the middle of the night before I go back to my empty hotel room.' And that is not the case here."

I could see from Jenny McCarthy Romo's delivery on this issue that it was an emotional connection for her. Where Michael Pearl was appropriately focused on their performance for his members, Jenny was helping with their needs as individual people on the ground in a strange town once the music stopped.

"An important part of the Pro Musica mission," I said, "is the development of the youth orchestra. We've talked some about that, but would you like to embellish on it a bit more?"

"What's happened with it since we took it over from the municipio a year and a half ago, when it was five or six young people without instruments and no one to teach them, is that now we have forty young people in this orchestra. We have instrument donations from all kinds of people. We also have an instrument company that contributes. I think music is underappreciated in this country, so if you help somebody follow their dream in that direction you never know who they could become some day."

"Is Pro Musica looking for volunteers in any capacity?"

"We are. Soon we're going to start looking for someone who enjoys design work, who will work with our designer on the programs. Also, we can always use new ushers, and for people who want to volunteer we can find something for them."

"How about for musical instruction for instruments?"

"We are open to every possibility. There can never be too much help in this line of work."

"I suppose it's no coincidence that your programs mainly occur in the fall and winter. It must be easy to draw performers down here from cold climates."

"It is, but we always have the fear that the weather will interfere with flight arrivals. It's only happened once, but we don't have a way to reach people who have concert tickets. Still, artists love coming down here. In January and February many of them end up staying for a week."

"Do you ever imagine yourself onstage up there on concert nights?"

"Never, although I have stood in for Michael Pearl making introductions several times. I was super nervous at first, but then I got better at it. But no, I don't like standing up in front of groups of people."

"Who would be your dream performer?"

"I don't know. We've had so many amazing performers, and I mean big names. I'm not sure I know enough about music today to say."

"The person reading your story and this book today is one imagining herself or himself in your shoes. They're wondering how that would work, to take a different fork in the road, to stretch out a bit more than their peers. What would you say to someone earlier in life, like yourself, who is thinking about that? Is it only an unusual kind of person who can do this?"

She nodded quickly. "I think it may be, John. My friends in college, the ones I still talk to, they've said to me, all of them at some point, 'I just don't think I could ever live in a foreign country. What do you do when you need a glass measuring cup?'"

We looked at each other for a while. Was this what it all really boiled down to? I'm not always looking for a bottom line in books like this, but sometimes it can just come right up on you with no warning. Some things can have a symbolic value you would never predict. But Jenny wasn't finished.

"It does kind of take a special person to do it forever. But come for a year, just to see life outside of the U.S. boundaries. Just do it."

CHAPTER TWELVE
KAY LYNNE SATTLER

Mexiquito is a neighborhood, or colonia as they're called here, on the northern edge of San Miguel. To the east it borders on Colonia Obraje and the Fabrica Aurora, the old shirt and fabric mill complex that's been adapted into an upscale art and antiques center. Late on a Sunday morning in June I was on my way there to talk to Kay Lynne Sattler, a ceramics artist who had moved here from Hawaii about a year earlier. We had chosen a Sunday because it was a quiet day to tape an interview in an area that was hopping with both new construction and renovation. Mexiquito feels like a community on the move.

Kay Lynne and her husband are two of the renovators. She and I sat at a round table in the unfinished living room. A hand-chiseled wiring channel skittered up the wall next to the fireplace. Since the walls are all masonry here, wiring is usually set up like this, just carved into the surface and plastered over. Lined up in a recess on the street wall and across the fireplace mantel were about eight of her ceramic pieces. Two of them gleamed with real gold.

She is a woman of medium height with a trim and youthful build. From her manner you would not guess she was sixty. Her expression was lively and engaged as we talked. She had told me earlier that she had enjoyed the first of my mysteries, *Twenty Centavos*, which is centered on counterfeit Mayan ceramics.

"For a lot of expats," I began, "climate is a major consideration in moving to San Miguel. But you came here from Hawaii, from Maui I believe. Did climate enter into your decision at all? Or was it just something you didn't need to think about?"

"Originally I bought a one way ticket from Colorado to Maui, and that idea came from the cold weather of the Rocky Mountains. Climate is very important to me. I'd been living in Hawaii for thirty-five years and having a climate that is pretty much paradise all year around, so choosing to relocate and where was a big decision. The reason central México seemed appealing was the arid climate, where Maui is humid. I was looking forward to the idea of actually having a bit of variation in seasonal changes, but without the snow."

"Coming from Minnesota, I can sympathize with that. I always think we have only two seasons here, brown and green. The green one is just starting up now, with the return of the rains."

"I'm looking forward to the rain and seeing the

desert come alive and our very own cactus garden bloom. Spring is leaving along with the heat, and the cold is nowhere in sight." April and May are the hottest months here.

"Aside from that, what were your principal reasons for settling here?"

"More than anything, it was to experience a different culture; architecture, music, a new language, people, an entirely new landscape. From Maui to México, from beaches to mountains. It was all of these things, and to be able to walk everywhere, the freedom of not relying on a car for transportation. The idea of experiencing all of this was very attractive."

"Was that not the case on Maui?"

"Unless you are living in a small town, and you live directly in the center of town, you are going to need a car."

"And you weren't in town there?"

She nodded slowly. "I was in a small town for quite a few years, and that was enjoyable. I would imagine it was quite similar to any small town where you can walk to a market or to the bank or post office. But as Maui continued to grow those small areas became overpopulated and harder to live in. Now you need a car to get around the island."

"What process, and as I ask this I'm sitting here looking at some of your work, led you to choose the ceramic arts as your preferred medium?"

My gaze stopped on a vessel with a narrow opening. The surface patina spoke of smoky minerals and organic matter. It might've been recovered from an ancient Roman or Greek shipwreck, or the ashes of Pompeii or Herculaneum. Kay Lynne told me about the firing process. It had been fired in the ground, with the vessel packed in combustible material. Each element had contributed as it burned. Whether oxygen was sparse or plentiful contributed to the tone and texture of the variegated result.

"I come from a family of artists. My mother was a musician and a painter, as was my brother, so growing up we had paintbrushes in our hands from a very young age. We grew up listening to classical music and I always imagined I would enter the arts in some way. At first I thought I might be another painter, but it was in high school that I happened to have a young hip teacher who exposed every possible medium to her students. That's when I was introduced to clay and I discovered what my path in life would be. There was no turning back."

"What was that encounter about? Was it the texture, just the feel of it in your hands, squeezing it into different shapes between your fingers?"

"Yes! That is a big part of it. The way I approach clay is like having a relationship. Rolling coils of clay and building by hand while seeing vessels grow slowly within my presence is a process of deliverance for me. In the beginning stages of creating a vessel, I may have an initial concept for the inspired piece but as the days go by and the vessel takes form, the clay will 'speak' and impart it's own 'spirit' into the final shape. Clay always has the final word."

I connected immediately with this because in my own experience of both painting and writing I knew the element of 'intimacy' was critical. The reader wants to see the author on the page, and that had to be no less true that the owner of a Kay Lynne Sattler piece would want to feel the residual heat of her presence in his or her hands.

"I also paint, and I discovered that my relationship with paint is completely different than my relationship with clay. My paintings are loose and abstract, less restricting and forgiving than clay. Clay is a very different medium, and for me working with it is truly listening to clay, a meditative process. I think that's mainly why I'm attracted to it."

"And here in the high desert you don't have that much time before the clay starts to set up, isn't that right?"

"That's true and something I'm relearning here in this new climate. The tropics are humid and the clay takes time to dry. In central México I'm finding that I need to be mindful to ensure the top section of the vessel is moistened and well covered. The dry air here can work either for me or against me. When creating a large piece the drying time has to be the same throughout as much as possible. I cannot have a piece drying at the bottom and moist on the top because it will risk the chance of a hairline crack. When you're hand building and joining coils of clay together, that's where the vulnerability lies."

"Are you part of any movement in ceramics? Call it a school of thought?"

"No, for me it's more about methodology." Her smile suggested a mild distaste for the idea of using a more collective approach. "I've always been interested in the pottery of the indigenous peoples, and reviving that in a contemporary way. Recovering this methodology of uniting clay with fire is exciting to me. Clay taken from the earth, returned to the fire, and set free to tell the story."

I liked that cyclical idea of 'returning to the fire,' and the longer perspective it expressed. Everything in the earth had started there. "In the time you've been in San Miguel, have you found a supportive climate for your artwork here? For example, in terms of finding a market?"

"Very much. A market as well as a supportive climate from other artists, one which I have found to be absolutely wonderful."

"Is it more than you had in Maui?"

"I've been a professional artist since I was twenty and represented both nationally and internationally. The art community in San Miguel is different from anywhere else."

"And these other people supporting you are not necessarily ceramic artists?"

"No. What I have experienced is San Miguel de Allende is a very passionate and supportive art community. I think this comes from expats arriving and having the time in their lives to truly explore art. Depending on where this town's artists are in their career, they are supportive of one another. I haven't noticed many egos here. There's also a market for my work and I'm anxious to discover how my style might evolve towards uncovering an authentic voice in reaching a broader market."

"And you have a gallery to show in now."

"I had the pleasure of showing with Galería San Francisco in the heart of *el centro*. As serendipity would have it, while I was still on Maui I contacted a property listing in San Miguel regarding a rental. The owner of the rental property just happened to be the owner of Galería San Francisco. One thing led to another, and I didn't end up renting the property, but I was invited to join the gallery. It was thrilling to arrive in San Miguel and have immediate gallery representation. It was a grand year of gallery openings and fiestas. Now I'm switching gears and anticipating the new construction of my art studio and gallery."

"Which leads me to another question. In a year's

residence, has your style begun to change to reflect your new surroundings?"

"Dramatically. That brings up a story. About two months after arriving in San Miguel, I was offered an amazing studio space in a hacienda directly next door to our casita. I was transporting all my supplies and my tools in bags. I was unaware at that time of how the *basura* worked here, how the trash was picked up. I had all my bags sitting on the cobblestone walkway. It was forty years worth of tools. When I came back out of our casita, I looked down and the bags were gone. The *basura* truck had accidentally mistaken my bags of supplies and tools for trash and picked them up. I ran down the street after them, but it was too late. It was a sinking feeling. I may not have used all those tools, but they greeted me every day, and you know, you get accustomed to how they feel. Holding some of them in my hand was like holding the hand of a good friend.

"During the time this incident happened it was in August, and there was a lot of corn being harvested. Everywhere I walked there was corn on street corners and in all the markets. I thought, OK, I've got a studio, and I've got clay. I'm going to create something for México, I'll create a series in honor of maize. Maize is more than food, for the Mexican people *maíz* is life. I shucked the corn, I had leaves strewn across the studio floor and corn hung on the stone walls. And holding the corn, do you know how it felt in my hand? It was like holding a new tool." She went over to the mantel and returned with a sculptural piece. "It's not overly contrived where you can see every little kernel, but I used an ear of corn to paddle and shape this vessel."

It was an organic combination of corn profiles. From the top emerged two sets of dry leaves.

"This is part of my Ode to Maíz. I created six in this series and premiered them at Galería San Francisco. They were well received, which was very humbling. At that moment when I lost my tools, my style radically changed, and it has continued to move more towards shapes being spontaneous and naturally organic. No doubt México will offer up unimaginable adventures for me with clay."

"Then let's go back even further than México. What kind of artistic journey has it been to the place in your art where you are now, from the point where you started?"

"In the very start of my career I was creating traditional clay shapes inspired by the pottery of the Native American women that I had seen in the Southwest as a little girl. When I moved to Hawaii, being surrounded by fire and water and sun, not to mention all the deities, I wanted a dramatic contrast to the primitive fired vessels to represent those elements. I experimented with paints, and other techniques, but the result of the applications seemed to be flat and lifeless sitting on the surface. I had no desire to become involved in glazes; and I wanted my works to remain natural from start to finish. That was when I discovered precious metals. Gold leaf is a natural element that's so incredibly rich, and a mere one hundred millionth of an inch thick. It is so thin that the slightest breath will carry it away. Precious metal has this delicate layering which gives the appearance of "being of the piece, not on the piece." And the beauty of course, is that it glows in the faintest of light. It's fabulous.

"It was about ten years into my career on Maui that my signature use of precious metals was introduced. I brought along with me to México all of my gilding materials and precious metals. While México loves her gold and silver, I'm not quite sure how the metals will be introduced to my new work."

"Of course," I said, "the part of México where we're sitting right now is silver country. There's silver leaf too."

"Yes, and I have a palladium which also does not need to be sealed, and it's very sensuous."

"So where do you go from here? Can you speculate on that?"

"In regards to art, now that my husband and I have been here one year, I have an opportunity, especially in our new casa, to just stop and listen to what México whispers to me. I know I will continue to feel inspired by nature and my surroundings. It will be interesting to see what the next chapter is, because to be honest, I really have no idea what the clay will ask of me."

"I like the idea of listening in that context because our surroundings can tell us so much. In that year has San Miguel started to feel like home to you?"

"San Miguel felt like home the minute my feet touched México. It was immediate, as soon as I got off the plane. It was effortless, from the moment we came to visit. We did a ten-day vacation to see if we might want to relocate here. From day one, the answer was unanimous. We returned to Maui and put our home on the market, sold everything in nine months, bought a couple of one-way tickets and arrived with two suitcases and a cat. Now that we've just celebrated one year in San Miguel, and we're going to be moving into our own home, I know it will begin to feel even more like home because little by little we'll be building our nest."

"Can you give me a few points of contrast between the Maui culture that you left and that of central México?"

"Yes, in regard to the Polynesian culture in Hawaii there are many similarities with the Mexican culture. The Polynesians are generous and welcoming. The men greet and embrace each other, and fathers spend a lot of time with and taking care of their children. Both are very happy cultures and entirely focused on family.

It seems to genuinely be all about helping each other. When we arrived here in San Miguel we were astonished by the same feeling of warmth."

"Are you missing anything about Hawaii?"

"I can honestly say we have never looked back. However, my husband and I were both just talking the other day about how we miss our gardens and Maui's produce. Hawaii is one of the few places in the world that has a perfect climate combined with the rich volcanic soil. With the many microclimates and ideal weather, you can grow all year around, and the taste and size of the produce is unbelievable. Hawaii's produce, I admit, is the one thing I do miss."

"How different is the cost living here?"

Her eyes grew larger. "Hawaii is the most expensive state in the nation, followed by New York and California. And it's the most isolated landmass in the world; about 2500 miles from the U.S. mainland."

"Everything has to be brought in except the produce."

"Yes! Everything has to be shipped or flown in, and that includes additional produce. Milk, for example can cost five dollars for half a gallon. And oddly enough we were paying six dollars for local organic bananas. Gas, electricity, and rent are all high. Of course the cost of property is also very high. That's the price for paradise. And this is kind of funny: Hawaii also has the most expensive toilet paper in the world. So, with the Hawaiian Islands behind us now, we are very grateful for the opportunity to live and experience México. It has become our new paradise."

I had not anticipated this and made a note to possibly explore toilet paper prices elsewhere in subsequent interviews. It might be a key cultural indicator, or just a crazy Hawaiian quirk. "Here's my windup question. As both a painter and a writer over many years, there's a core belief that I've come to embrace: A creative life trumps all other options and offsets all, or at least most of life's vicissitudes. Does your experience support this?"

Kay Lynne gave me a wry smile. "I think that clay chose me, and I've thought about that a lot." She leaned forward at the table. "There was a period in my life when I stopped working with clay, thinking, what if I had my own little tour business on Maui? I recall taking a long hike with my brother up to a very high point on the island to watch the sun set. I had kind of an epiphany at that moment, and that was to totally commit my life to clay. It was the clay that was always calling me. I realized that when I was not creating, then I was thinking about creating, and when I was creating, I found it nearly impossible to think about anything else."

I made an encouraging gesture, but said nothing more.

"But back to your question; I think really

participating in life, whatever that might mean for each of us, is the key. Everyone has the ability to be creative, to be able to express themselves authentically through what they love to do, and that is a gift."

A few minutes later I said goodbye to Kay Lynne Sattler, pressing her hand and giving her a hug as I went out to my car. There is a subtle connection among people in the arts, even when the media are totally different. I can't always explain it.

The street was still quiet, possibly resting for a Monday morning outburst of construction. I haven't known many ceramic artists and she had left me with some strong impressions. One was her commitment to her craft and materials. To her, the sensuous quality of moist clay was like words are to the writer. Her stress on the relationship that involved felt right on as I listened, and it still does as I work on this chapter.

She also possessed a skill that most artists need but not so many have: a good head for business.

CHAPTER THIRTEEN
SUE LEONARD & JÓVENES ADELANTE

The road to Querétaro (officially the Salida a Querétaro,) climbs a long hill from the el centro district of San Miguel. After leveling out it circles the roundabout at the libramiento (the ring road) and goes on past the Tuesday Market and further toward Querétaro, our neighboring capital of the state of the same name about an hour away. It is clearly an old royal road that centuries ago served the same function it does today.

Near the spot where it levels out stands a U-shaped two-story strip mall optimistically called Plaza Primavera, the Plaza of Spring, with two rows of parking in the center. A Volkswagen dealer hopefully anchors one end of it. Next to the Beetles and the Passats my dentist had his practice for quite a few years; he was a technical expert who could construct an excellent bridge. At one inner corner is the company that still furnishes my car insurance. The rest of the businesses are equally mundane. In this great historic and romantic town, one that the tourists think is all mariachis and girls in off-the-shoulder tops with flowers pinned in their hair, this plaza is a place where most people wouldn't linger once their business was done. Because of that, Plaza Primavera is all the more necessary. It is dedicated to the most ordinary needs of San Miguel residents, except, that is, for a pair of small offices tucked into a mostly untraveled spot on the second floor. Who would guess that in such a nondescript corner is a business that deals exclusively in dreams? It's called Jóvenes Adelante; approximately, Youth Forward.

I've known about it since the first week I arrived in San Miguel late in the summer of 2007. My wife and I were invited to dinner by two old-time residents, Virginia and Farley Wheelwright, and that was our first local social engagement. One of the subjects that came up during that evening was Jóvenes Adelante. Our hostess, Virginia, talked about their program of putting worthy local kids through college. Kids who showed promise and determination, but would never stand a chance of financing it, even though it doesn't cost a great deal of money by expat standards.

We were only in the initial stages of getting settled, but even then I could tell it was a wonderful project. So early in our tenure I hadn't thought much about it yet, but what I came to realize over time was that one aspect of settling into San Miguel as an expat was the question of engagement. Most expats who move to San Miguel are retired, but this does not feel like a place where they expect to kick back and watch life pass them by from their front porch, not that we have them here, at least not on the main floor. Nor at 6400 feet elevation, is this the beach. From years of watching the people around me I know that living here is more about doing than merely being.

For a man who has owned or managed a small business, or a woman who has finished a professional career, a blank page presents itself on arrival. What would generate a meaningful experience as a replacement for an earlier vocation? The idea of giving something back is not a cliché; it lies at the essence of how people can continue to employ a lifetime of accumulated capabilities. What you know from forty years of interaction in a business or professional practice in your previous community cannot easily be taught here, but it can be *applied* in your dealings with people trying to gain a foothold at the other end of their lives.

Other expats might arrive in San Miguel with a background in a service position, perhaps education or medicine. To seek out a means of continuing in that vein would be natural, as I was about to discover upstairs at the Plaza Primavera.

Some observers have said that México combines the characteristics of a third-world country with those of a first world country. One situation that I see as capable of great improvement is education. Public schooling is free and compulsory in this state of Guanajuato only through middle school. High school costs money and although it is not at all expensive by expat standards, it is still beyond the means of many parents even if they would like to help their children do better than they did. And beyond that, for most students the mere idea of going to college is no more than a fantasy.

Among the many NGOs (non-government organization), more than a hundred that deliver a wide range of services here, one is Jóvenes Adelante. I had done a magazine article about them several years ago, and I wanted to catch up with them again to answer several new questions. What kind of person gets involved with their activities? Since they fund higher education at an individual level, it is obvious that they run on financial donations. Anyone can write a check, and many do, but what are the other ways an expat can play a role at a personal level?

Their program is life changing, since having a college degree opens doors that would otherwise remain closed. Furthermore, having a college graduate in the family usually raises the condition of every member of that family; so making college possible has a reverberating effect like the pebble tossed into a quiet pool. The graduate will often go on to mentor and financially assist other family members.

I asked a friend who was working with Jóvenes Adelante if he could suggest a person who could bring me up to date. He offered the name of Sue Leonard, and we arranged a meeting at her office. I have already described where I found it. I pulled up in my eleven-year-old Ford Edge SUV, a vehicle that I have always known was too wide for these streets, and I have to say, some of those younger and trimmer Volkswagens looked kind of hot as I passed.

I found a staff of three upstairs in the main part of the office. Sue Leonard came in a moment later and we set up a recorded conversation in the adjacent conference room.

Sue is a lively person of retirement age who has obviously failed to discover any reason at all to retire. Not that she seems to be looking very hard, since there is a certain grace and ease in her manner. We got started almost immediately, seated at their long conference table.

"Earlier you furnished me with some background information that addressed your beginnings as a nurse practitioner in a children's healthcare clinic in Colorado, one that had been poorly served. Then there was a stint in the Peace Corps in Fiji with your husband. That was followed by living and working in Cambodia, Africa, Azerbaijan, and Central Asia after the Peace Corps. If I wanted to suggest a single word to summarize your working life it would have to be *service*. Would that be very far off the mark?"

She laughed at this. "Not too far. You did a good job."

"Is that a philosophy of life as much as a type of occupation? It's such a powerful thread running through your history."

"You're right, it is. I hadn't thought much about it until you put it that way, but yes, of course, I'm not really happy unless I'm doing something that contributes to the universe."

"Over the years has there been more of an emphasis on the field of health, or on education?"

"Health is my career, but when I came to San Miguel it was nice to do something different. It was fun for me to get into education and learn what it was like here. I had been a school nurse during that time as well, so I'd had my feet in education. It was especially fun to be here and look at education from the Mexican perspective and learn what that means. I have to say it's been quite eye-opening."

"I'm sure it was. During your travels was your husband involved in similar service positions?"

"That's interesting and you've made me think about that. He was a banker in his business career, but all the way through, even early in on when he was a young man in his mid to late thirties, he was involved in black/white workshops during the racial crisis in Louisiana.

These were sessions that brought the leaders of the black and white communities together. They would sit down, usually for two or two and a half days to try to work out the issues they had. There would be the more radical black leaders, as well as more moderate ones. There was also the police force and the social services people. It dealt with a lot of the racial tensions in Baton Rouge."

"Would that have been in the sixties?"

"Right. The late sixties and into the seventies. In addition to that he was on a lot of nonprofit boards over the years. This is the second marriage for both of us. When we got together he was in banking and we decided that, after some changes in our lives, we wanted to work overseas. The Peace Corps was the best way to do that."

"So you didn't go into the Peace Corps right out of college."

"No, I was accepted, but I married my first husband instead. I had always wanted to go, so when the opportunity came later, we went."

"There are other people I've talked to in this book who have traveled a great deal and have lived in widely varying parts of the world. Travel has influenced their view of where or what home is, a subject that runs as a thread through this narrative. Was there one place where you lived, or even several, that seemed especially like home?"

She shook her head slowly. "Not so much. We

tended to live in very different kinds of cultures. Fiji is phenomenally different, and Cambodia was our next long residence. We came in after the Pol Pot era. That was quite a dramatic time to be there. As many people who have worked in other countries will tell you, the first place you go is the one you connect with at a heart level. For us, that was Fiji, of course. Our focus was not on deliverables, it was on getting to know the culture. That was our job, so we got to spend our energy doing that. And, we had fascinating work to do that let us get very deep into the indigenous civilization. Fiji was the best."

"Deliverables is not a word I recognize in this context. Can you clarify that?"

"Sure, in the international development world, especially if projects are funded by USAID (U.S. Agency for International Development), all projects and programs must accomplish specific goals relative to that project. They must deliver what they promised to do with the funds provided."

"So it's about accountability. Do you have a strong knack for languages?"

She shook her head slowly. "I have zero knack. In my next life, that's what's going to happen."

"You'll be an instantaneous translator at the U.N."

"Absolutely! It means that I have some very basic skills in a lot of different languages that I've mostly forgotten now."

"After all that travel through so many countries, what was it about San Miguel that made you stop here, if you have indeed stopped?"

"Yes, we have stopped here. While we were out in the world we checked out every place we could. We looked at Hawaii when we were coming back from Fiji because that would keep us in the South Pacific culture. We also checked out Costa Rica and Croatia and the Dominican Republic. Then there was Portugal, and we threatened to look at Malta. Every place we were—of course, Thailand and New Zealand—we checked out other places around there, always looking for the perfect place. At one point we decided that México was a real possibility. We came and spent nine months traveling around the country to see if we could find that perfect place."

"What exactly were you looking for that would fit that description?" In my work I've had to come up with a lot of different words to describe México, most of them positive, but I have rarely used *perfect* as an adjective.

"We were looking for a place that was on the coast and in the mountains. There aren't many of those where you can walk to the beach from your front door."

"No." The nearest beach is eight hours from here by car.

"So on that trip we decided San Miguel was

the place we wanted to be. Then we went back over to Azerbaijan, then the Dominican Republic, and we were getting ready to leave and Bob said, 'I've got to go back to San Miguel and see how it compares.'

"I had to go to the States for some medical things and he called me and said, 'OK, I've found a house on the Querétaro Road and two in Los Frailes, so we have the country and we have the city. We're good to go.' It's close to grandkids, and it's a fascinating combination because there's a lot of the indigenous culture as well as the Spanish culture. Both of them are so alive here. We're at that magical place in México where they fit together. This country also has so many subcultures that it's a fascinating place to live. Then, of course, it's also quick to travel to the U.S. and easy to connect with family. The cost of living is decent, and then there's the weather. The expat population is also very interesting."

"And then there is Jóvenes Adelante," I said. Sitting in their conference room we were surrounded by file cabinets, ledgers, stacks of white plastic nesting chairs, and a wall that is now filled and overflowing onto the opposite one with photos of all the local students that are graduates of this program. "So, you've been volunteering here about how long?"

"It's been ten years, and like many volunteers I've come and gone. Sometimes I've been intensively involved, and then I've stepped back a bit and done more overseas work. And then I've come back again."

"Have you seen a lot of changes in that period?"

"What do you think?"

"Is it mainly growth?"

"No. You know, the organization started with a tiny little group of people gathered around a coffee table saying, literally, 'Well, one of our friends is helping this kid get through school. Aren't there some other kids who also need help?' They decided they would raise money to fund some others."

"When was that?"

"That was in 2001. In 2007 there was a major change, and at that point the original group decided this could be bigger, but in order to do that they would need to change how they did things. They would need some leadership. A woman we all knew said she would volunteer to be the president. That was Amanda Ruiz. She said we needed to bring in more kids and have a mentor program. We knew that one of the strengths of this program was that all of the people running it had kept in close contact with the kids, and we wouldn't be able to continue that if we made it bigger. We needed to figure out how to keep track of the kids and provide the one-on-one support they needed. So Amanda started the mentor program."

"You would bring people on exclusively to work as mentors."

"Exactly, and that has continued and even become the cornerstone of what we do. All of these kids have had one person who was important to them. It's always a neutral person who is not family, so if the family is doing something crazy, they can talk to this person. They're not roommates, so if their roommate is doing something crazy, they can talk to this person. And they're not professors, either."

"It's a situation where being an outsider matters."

"Exactly."

"So these mentors tend to be mature. They bring their business or at least, their life experience to the situation of their assigned student. Their relationship is individual and particular."

"It's very particular. In the early years a lot of the kids had mentors who didn't speak much Spanish, and they didn't have much English, so they just muddled through. Now we have more and more mentors who are either bilingual or Spanish speakers. Preferably bilingual; it just makes the whole thing easier."

"Are you advocating too that the students learn some English?"

"We've always done that, but it can frequently be a struggle. The kids often don't have much appreciation for how important English can be for them until the last year of college. At that point they're looking ahead, and suddenly asking themselves what they'll be doing when they get out. This year we're going to make a stronger push. Every year all the kids sign a contract, and each year it gets embellished. This year a clause in it will say they are committed to learn English. We are committed to make sure they have the resources they need to make that happen. We can see now how much stronger our English speaking graduates are and how much better they do than those who have no English skills."

"What would you tell people who are new to San Miguel about volunteering? Some are probably reading this and wondering whether it's a model for a lot of the volunteer work that goes on here."

"I've seen a lot of volunteers come through over the years. Some of the people who move here want to get involved with something right away. We have plenty of those kinds of volunteers. They show up and they say, 'I'm a volunteer. Give me a job.' And we still do that.

"Or sometimes they'll say, 'We want to be on your board.' Up until the last few years we have needed people to be on the board, and we said OK."

"Is that the ideal situation?"

"Not really. It works much better for the volunteers if they get settled into town first, building a house, or whatever they need to do. They should get to know the nonprofit groups in town, and there are many good ones."

"Rather than rushing in and saying, 'put me to

work.'"

"Right. Your work needs to match your passion, and you don't know where your passion lies until you get to know some of these organizations. Nor do you know the level of commitment you want to make. If you volunteer right away you are ignoring the fact that San Miguel has a lot of other things going on. Maybe you'd rather be going to concerts or lectures than being stuck doing the volunteer work you've committed to. It's better to wait a bit."

What sensible advice this was! "Is the board member's job mainly to raise funds?"

"No, ours is a working board, and in the early years they did everything. We had no staff then. You saw the current staff in the other office as you came in. They take on the day-to-day operations, and the board can do much more creative things. Two of the board members are working with the student programs people to manage all of the activities we do with the students, and there are many. The staff now backs up all of the work done by board members: financial record keeping, monitoring the overall administration, and of course raising funds and building strong relationships with donors, and developing communications with various aspects of the community. The students get a scholarship, and they get a computer and a mentor when they come in. We have a team of psychologists that provide psychological support for the kids as they manage what is a strange new world for them with many, many challenges. That started with expatriates but now all the psychologists are Mexican. We keep track of their grades and their school registration. If we see their grades start to drop then we contact one of the psychologists and say, 'You need to talk to this kid because something is wrong.'"

"Are those psychologists part of the screening process for admission?"

"Some of them help with that as well. We do an elaborate screening and we're into that phase now."

This conversation took place late in April.

"The cut off date for applications this year was March 4. We received 137."

"How many new students can you handle in the coming year?"

"Twenty-five is our goal. That has depended on how much money we've been able to raise. That part is going quite well this year. We screen the applications and get them down to fifty or sixty. Then we do interviews using two volunteers with each student. From that process we narrow it down to thirty-five or forty, and then we do home visits to all of their families, with both the kid and the parents present. And we don't supply all of the money. The parents have to come up with some of it, and the kids come up with some of it."

"Everybody is invested. What happens when the

family can't come up with their share?"

"We do have a special fund that we are raising money for now that will allow us to provide qualifying students with a larger scholarship that will enable us to take them into the program. In the past we've had to turn most of those students away and not even consider them for a scholarship. Even so, we always need to assure ourselves that the parents are committed to this curriculum in this university. Because when they are gone off to school, there is no extra money coming into the household from that child. And there is no help to be had from them if someone at home is sick. For many families, that is too much of a sacrifice."

"When I was sitting in the office earlier just before you arrived I was looking at a framed set of pictures on the wall with your 2014 admissions. There were nine of them, and six were women and three were men. Tell me about that proportion. Was it exceptional that year?"

"It's interesting when you look at all of these classes, because very consistently we have two-thirds women and one-third men."

"Why is that?"

"If the past some of the young men often went to the States to find work. Now they're not going as much. Is it because the young women are more focused? They know what they want and it is not to be a mom right now, which is their only other option."

This made sense. "It's a marvelous opportunity for young women in a society that has not been known for providing a lot of them. Someone once suggested to me that young women are more expendable from the family because they can't earn as much as young men."

"That's true, but they also provide the soft skills in the family. We've lost more than one potential student because there was a family member who was sick and needed care. That young girl was the one who provided it because no one else in the family was willing or able to step into that role."

"What is the overall staff here? How many people are engaged in this enterprise on a given day, including all the mentors, everyone."

"To start with there are four full time staff here in the office. Two are focused on direct student services. Our new executive director supervises the whole operation, and then Mayra, who met you at the door, fills in all the gaps and makes the Executive Director's job possible. Those are the paid staff. Then we have about seventy mentors, and some have charge of more than one student. There are eight people on the board, all volunteers. And there are some other assorted volunteers."

"So you're pushing a hundred people to make all this happen."

"Oh, easily. And now we're going to bring in twenty-five new students, which means we'll probably bring in fifteen new mentors. That's our goal, to bring in twenty-five a year."

"How many students are enrolled in your program and currently in school?"

"Right now the number is sixty-six. Students graduate throughout the year here so that number can be a moving target."

"What are the organization's current needs for volunteers?"

"We could use mentors and interviewers with at least some Spanish skills. Also people who can tutor English. In addition we need people who can help with social media or produce radio spots or short videos. Volunteers who could manage one-off fundraising events and those who could write promotional material, especially articles about students."

"I know that the way many people entering the workforce often find jobs here is through their family or similar connections. How do you deal with that for the students you mentor? Sometimes the university qualification isn't probably enough to get them smoothly into the kind of job they've studied for."

"It rarely is enough. That's a major problem for our kids who do not have those family connections. What does make a difference for them is that they are very bright and very motivated. Most of them are also quite driven. They excel in school and part of the school process here is that they have to do some social volunteering and they're also required to do an internship before they can get their credential."

"That must be useful."

"Incredibly useful, because if they have excelled in school they can get into some very good intern programs. If they do well at that internship they can sometimes walk out with a job. At the beginning of this program we had a lot of kids going into architecture and law. Those are very fine careers, but unless you have an uncle who's an architect or lawyer with a firm set up that you can go to work in, you'll have trouble. You can end up driving a taxi."

"Right, because you are not going to go out and start your own architectural firm from scratch. What has kept you associated with Jóvenes Adelante this long?"

"It is a joy and very gratifying to see these frightened young people grow up into capable and strong adults able to support themselves and their families. That never stops being exciting for me."

"What is your personal goal for your association with JA? You said you have reenlisted as president."

"It's to get it more and more sustainable. For me, of course, the reward is seeing the phenomenal growth that has happened over the years. It has turned into a very strong organization that continues through the work of many people. We've got a bit more effort to make on

the staff, and more to do on the board to get
tainability there, but we are very close. It should a
a place where it can have a life of its own."

After chatting for a while longer about less con-
sequential matters, I said goodbye to Sue Leonard and
found my way back down the stairs to the twelve or fourteen car parking area enclosed by the Plaza Primavera.
The thought that stuck in my mind was that on that day,
Jóvenes Adelante was putting sixty-six kids through college, kids that almost certainly could never have made it
through college on their own, or, in all likelihood, even
started. In the coming fall term, they were gearing up to
bring on twenty-five more. If the point of an organization like this is to make a difference, I couldn't think of a
better route to take.

There are more than one hundred such organizations operating in San Miguel. I could've picked almost
any of them for this book. My reasons for overlooking
any of them were mostly chance, and not based on merit
or careful scrutiny. The truth is that I could easily do an
entire book on that subject alone.

The scale of the San Miguel community is small
enough so that any dedicated individual can make an
observable and measurable difference. This is not true
of every place you might choose to live. Although stars
are welcome, you do not need to be one to matter to this
community and to reward yourself. The task of anyone

d is to first do his or her home-
)r engagement are almost too
· there is one or more opportu-
)assion of anyone who merely
l, one person at a time.

CHAPTER FOURTEEN
DEBORAH AXTON

Across from my house, on the southern edge of the Río Laja valley, the hamlet of San Miguelito winds along the contoured bluff. Behind it a number of small ranchos provide boarding for horses and some hit and miss agriculture. Over the intractable white stone of the plateau, the topsoil is only about ten to twenty inches deep on average, so plowing is chancy, as is the rainfall. Here Martina, my wife's Lusitano mare, lives with her equine friends, more than thirty in all, plus six dogs, a dozen chickens, several falcons and a few sheep. Two ranchos down from her is the spread belonging to Deborah Axton.

Deborah is the widow of Hoyt Axton, the actor, singer and songwriter who died in 1999. Although he wrote in a variety of genres from country and folk to rock, in his song titled *Evangelina*, his material dealt with what he called "Old México." Although I didn't see the subject come up again, that made me wonder if he had a connection to this place and how it might differ from hers, since about nineteen years after his passing in Montana, this is where she has come to earth much of the time. Because this area and the adjacent village of Atotonilco is the site where the War of Independence began in 1810, it could uniquely be called Old México.

I drove down a single lane dirt road and stopped near the end along a white wall about twelve feet high with a black iron gate. When I pulled up it swung open. I was expected.

Inside was the paddock area with stables, a ring, and all the equine necessities. Further down was a cluster of several casitas in blue and green. That was where I parked. One of the grooms trotted down with me and waved back a pack of dogs.

Deborah Axton came out to greet me. She had just returned from riding and was wearing jeans and a straw cowboy hat. We decided to move further back from the paddock to limit the noise, which my recorder picks up most minutely. We settled at a small round table with an umbrella. She's of average height with a trim and active figure. Through blue eyes her gaze is frank and friendly, but unflinching.

"What a charming place this is! How many horses can you keep here?"

"I have nine and they're all comfortable. There's no shortage of anything. They each have their own corral and water and cover. And they've each got their own stall at night." Her accent is pure Texas. She was raised in Fort Worth.

"Are they friends?"

"Well, they're good friends on the trail. They get along here when they're next to each other. The two fillies play together and that's about it."

"I suppose riding must be one of your passions. What are your others?"

"Riding my horses is definitely a passion of mine. It has been since I was three years old. As for other passions, music has always been one. I think music is the harmonic convergence that brings us all together. The tones of music are so important for the soul. It's an inner vibration. Music is an important part of our lives, to recognize and appreciate the tones, the sounds."

"Are you a musician yourself?"

"No, I'm not. I always loved biking. I like to ride ten miles a day. I try to do that three days a week. I like to kayak, too. I just did a kayaking competition in Querétaro where we did eight kilometers. I completed it and won first place in my category, but the problem was that I was the only one my age in that category. But I completed it." She gave me a broad grin.

"Now the people reading this are wondering how old you are."

"I'll be sixty-five this year." She showed no hesitation in acknowledging this. "I believe it's our responsibility to take care of ourselves and our health. If we want to be physically healthy we need to be physically active. If we want to be mentally healthy we have to be mentally active. Spiritually it's the same. It's important to have a strong spirituality, good physical health, a good mental state, and then be grateful and blessed each day, because there are no guarantees."

"Is this part of México a special place for you spiritually?"

"I think it is."

"I know that we're sitting here on a plateau composed of crystals. In a dense white matrix a lot of the stone is a translucent amber, pale green, and light red."

"I've never been into crystals and their vibrations, but I think that where we are is definitely a healing place. Everybody has their own feelings, their own philosophical and spiritual beliefs. I believe that angels are everywhere here and that spirits who have passed over stay around. I don't believe there is much that is evil here. I feel there is a lot of goodness in this country. I also believe that in this part of México there is a sweetness that I haven't experienced before as consistently as this until I came here."

I looked at her for a moment. It did not seem to me that what she was talking about was a good match for the Old México of Hoyt's single song on the subject, but I didn't want to interrupt her train of thought.

"You told me in an earlier conversation that you

have another home in Montana, but to me this feels like a place where you could come to earth, perhaps the way you would after a strenuous journey, or even an unsettled life. Is one place more like home than the other? If it is, what makes it home? Some people have said their stuff is part of that, but in the case of the Montana place, could it be the memories?"

"Well yes, I think that Montana is home too. Hoyt, my late husband, and I moved there from Los Angeles. Because we lived up there I still have a love for that state, its people and its lifestyle. If I were going to live in the United States, Montana would be my home. But I was born and raised in Fort Worth, Texas. I lived out in California for a long time, and I loved it. I think some of the nicest people I've ever met come from Southern California. But in coming to San Miguel in 2003, after Hoyt passed away in 1999, I realized I had lost my purpose when he died. After taking care of him after his stroke in 1995, and after he passed away, I was lost up there. In 2003 my brother asked me to come down here for Day of the Dead. I flew to Fort Worth and met him with a mutual friend."

"Was that visit in this area?"

She nodded slowly as if seeing it again. "It was in San Miguel, but we came in this way through Atotonilco." Her gesture took in the enclosed *ranchito* where we sat and the village below it. "And as we drove in I felt that one day I was going to live out here. Not exactly knowing how or when, but I felt I was going to be here in this area. I was drawn here from the highway immediately the first time driving in. Later I went down to Patzcuaro (in the state of Michoacán) for Day of the Dead, then came back through here and went back to Montana and made arrangements. When I was still here I rented a room, it was in November. It was getting really cold and I chose to come back down here for the winter."

"That was your first winter getaway from Montana?"

"Right. So I rented an apartment in town at the Hotel Sautto on Hernandez Macias. I kept that for two years. While I had that as a base I found a piece of land to buy in Atascadero, at the top edge of San Miguel, and built a house. It was a beautiful house, and the contractor did a fabulous job building it. I mostly stayed in Montana while they worked on the house, everything was easy."

"But you didn't end up there? It sounds wonderful. I can just imagine the views."

"Well yes, however, I am not a city girl. What I learned is that I can no longer have people living right next to me. I need my privacy, I don't like living next door to anyone ever. So I found this little place where we're sitting now next to Atotonilco. And the finish work wasn't even done on the house in town then. I mean I was living in it, but they were still finishing up on the detail of the house. And then I found this, the place I'm in now. It's not fancy, but it was perfect for me. The minute I saw it I went, 'Hoyt, you would love this.'"

"I can see that so well. It looks like the Old West."

With a wistful look she paused for a moment as she listened to some noises from the paddock, then shook her head. "You know, I've had big and I've had fancy, and I'm just not into any of that anymore, but I fell in love with it. It was a tough sell here in San Miguelito to win respect from the local people. It was important to me because I feel it's an honor to live here. It was also important to earn their good will, and to live in their little village."

"I drive this village main street most days," I said. "I know the little yellow *tienda* where the local guys buy their liter bottles of beer and drink it sitting on the stone curb. We call that spot the town square, but it's no more than a speed bump on a one and a half lane road. Down a bit is the rolled up wire fence where the goatherd lets his goats out every day to stroll down into the valley for literally better pastures."

"Yes, and it's about all the beautiful children that we pass candy to on our horse rides, the sweet loving mothers, the ones we buy our fresh juice from every morning, and all the wonderful families. It's their acceptance I cherish and respect..."

These were the people whose respect Deborah

had wanted to earn. I was sure she had, just as I was also sure they had no idea whatever where she'd come from or the kind of life she had led.

"What were you doing before and where was Hoyt in his career when you met him? I can imagine you were on your own path then."

"I had been with another musician for sixteen years and we had just separated. When we split up, a mutual friend of ours, the actor Jan-Michael Vincent, asked me to come over one evening. He told me someone was there who wanted to meet me. I went over and it was Hoyt Axton. I had dinner at Jan and Joanne's, and I met Hoyt when he was sitting outside looking at the ocean. I took him a plate of food and I sat down with him outside, just the two of us. That was it, and I never left him again until I lowered him into the ground."

A long delicate silence followed. The dogs had found something passing by outside the gate that was more interesting than we were. The powerful single sentence summary of a ten-year connection that Deborah had offered me left little to add. You can have these conversations with people you know slightly but not long or deeply, and they will suddenly offer you a conclusion they spent years arriving at. They quietly open their palm and there it is. When that happens it always feels like a gift.

"What year would that have been when you met him?" I said, for lack of something more profound.

"That was in 1990."

"In my own youth I spent a lot of time at the edges of the music business in San Francisco. I was doing promotional brochures for singers and writing song lyrics, and I know that just being around that scene can be a wild ride. Was that the case with Hoyt?"

"Yes, and that's the reason he died at sixty-one. Absolutely. He had everything he wanted at his fingertips. There were people who would give him anything. It would be drugs, literally anything he wanted. It was that kind of life every day. If you lived on the edges of the music business you understand that you have to be really strong in order to survive it."

I'd had friends in San Francisco who had died of heroin overdoses, extremely talented people who left us in their thirties and forties.

"Hoyt would come home and get clean and sober."

"After being on the road?"

"Yes, and then he would go off again. I didn't go with him all the time. Once we left Los Angeles and moved to Montana I pretty much stayed home. We had dogs and horses, and I was selling real estate. If he was going to Fort Worth or Los Angeles, I would go. But to anyplace else he went on his own with the band."

"Do you think he would've been surprised that he didn't live any longer than he did?"

She managed a small shrug. "I think he was surprised that he had lived as long as he did. He told me that one of the reasons he loved me was that I had come into his life, and otherwise he would've been pushing up daisies way before he was."

"Did that lifestyle wear you down?"

"No! Because I didn't get involved with it. I had already been at the edges of it for seventeen years before we got together. I know how it goes with everything you want, every vice you might have. You can have money, you can have cocaine, you can have anything you want, any time. I learned at a pretty young age that I had to have my own discipline. And I learned that I wanted to work. I got pregnant at seventeen because of unfortunate circumstances at home. I was looking for a way out. I didn't get a college education; I didn't even finish high school. But I have never been afraid to work. I would get up every morning and go to work. I worked for the bookstore in Malibu, Books and Company. I worked for a clothing store. I worked for ICM for about a minute and couldn't stand it. I hated it and quit."

"Can I ask you what that company was?"

"International Creative Management."

"It's a talent agency."

"Yes, but it was just not my cup of tea. I didn't like driving into Beverly Hills every day from Malibu. It did not work for me. Phillip and I were together for sixteen years. He moved his band from Fort Worth to Los Angeles. I came out there and it was the nonstop sex, drugs and rock 'n' roll scene in Malibu in the eighties. I'm grateful I survived it and that I kept a day job, one where I did something to give me a purpose and a way to get away from that scene. I'd get home from work at six o'clock and everybody was just getting up and eating breakfast. So later, seeing it again wasn't that tough. I already knew how tough it was when I met Hoyt."

"He must've understood or at least sensed your need to define a different kind of lifestyle for yourself in that relationship."

Deborah put her hand down flat on the table and leaned toward me. "I think what Hoyt realized was that I was a hard-headed Texas woman and I was not going to conform to anything that was going to strip away my spirit and my soul. It was not going to happen."

Overhead a straggle of six white egrets rode the thermals over us and into the Laja valley. My eyes followed them for a moment, although they showed no interest in us.

"There is definitely a honky-tonk element to some of Hoyt's songs. Was that a costume he put on? Who was he when he let his hair down once the music stopped?"

Her left hand brushed this idea aside. "I know what you're saying, but he was the very same person.

What you saw onstage was what I saw at home. He always had a pad and pen with him. He would write down every thought. He would sing to me all the time. And he was funny; he always had a great sense of humor. He was a brilliant artist and songwriter. And a thinker, too. It was a wonderful experience to share some time with him."

Of course I already knew that he came by the songwriting talent honestly, since his mother had co-written *Heartbreak Hotel* for Elvis Presley.

"What would he think of your situation here today? In fact, what has been your journey from Montana to México? Did you two ever talk about living down here? If not, how did it come about that you did?"

"No, we never talked about it. We went to México only one time. We were in Cabo; it was a fishing trip. He was miserable. He was hot and he couldn't stand it. I never thought about central México as a place to live until I came down here after he was gone. But Hoyt would've loved it here."

"Of course at 6400 feet this is a totally different climate from the beaches."

"In his songs, México was only a story, you're right, but he was a storyteller. He respected and appreciated México being so different from the U.S. My own roots here might have come from one of my grandfathers. He was a flight trainer at the Air Force academy. I know he spent some time in jail in Guadalajara because he was also a bootlegger. Every year he and my grandmother came through Fort Worth on the way to Guadalajara. My other grandfather was called Curly. He was totally bald and kind of a hobo that we used to pick up and drop off at the fright yard in Fort Worth. I guess my fearlessness comes from them."

"Hoyt's been gone now for nineteen years. How have you changed since then? Who are you now, and what has happened to you since his passing?"

"What I have done is I've grown up." She placed her hand on my forearm as if to underline this statement. "I have learned to trust my decisions. I've grown up to know that a partner is wonderful to have in your life, but it doesn't make me what I am, and not having one doesn't break me either. I could have a dog rescue, I could have privacy, and I've found it out there. I came from a harsh beginning and this is my safe haven."

Her statement was perfectly underlined by our surroundings. "Has your view of the U.S. changed as you lived here?"

"Not at all. I am proud to be an American, and I say that with total honesty. I love our country. But still, it's a place with a lot of political issues going on right now that I'm not interested in. I hate the division. The division in our country is a heartbreak to me, but I don't have to deal with that down here. I vote in Montana and I am active politically, but I find my peace here. I find the sweetness of this country much easier on my person than being in the U.S. But having said that, I still love America."

"It's sad what relations between the two countries have become now."

"That's almost the worst part, all this talk about the wall and sending troops to the border. I take pride in living in this little village of San Miguelito."

"The people who are reading your story in this book all have their own stories as diverse as any I could ever come up with. Some of them are looking at you, at your horses and your rescue dogs, your cluster of casitas near the edge of a tiny river in the mountains of central México, they're looking at you with amazement, or with the sense that they could never do this themselves. Others are feeling a small nudge from it. They are less challenged by the idea of it. The words, 'You know, I could damn well do that, too, if I decided to,' are forming as an unconscious whisper on their lips. They turn and look quickly over their shoulder to see that no one heard them say it. What would you say today, after this long journey you have taken, to anyone who is now reading this? And OK, even finding a certain charm in it?"

She gave me a broad smile. "Well, John, it's like the Nike commercial. Just do it! I didn't know a soul down here. I didn't even know where the *jardín* (the main plaza) was in San Miguel. Sure, I got down here and had a WTF moment. Absolutely I did. It was like, 'What have I done?' But then I did it little by little from there, minding my own business. I met some people who were helpful and guided me, and I fell in love with México." She paused and considered this for a long moment. "And you know, anyone can do it if they want to. I've brought people out here to ride horses and they'll say things like, 'Are you in the Witness Protection Program or something? You're so far out in the middle of nowhere.'

"But I much prefer this. I've never been afraid to have a new experience. I'll travel anywhere. If I want to go I'll just go. I know I'm capable of working, I've never been afraid to work. I'll scrub toilets in order to pay my bills. I'm not above doing anything that will allow me to have the peace, and to live the life that I choose."

That seemed like a clear enough place to end this conversation. Nothing else I could ask her was likely to top that statement. I got up from the table and shook her hand. I know we both felt she had told me exactly what she wanted to tell me about herself and her journey into central México. But Deborah Axton's voyage seemed to be one that was devoid of any sentimentality.

My own sense of México matched that well. I do love the mood of a good old time ballad, and I love the mariachis in their embroidered pants and high boots, but at the end of the day, any day, the reality of this country needs to be taken straight up. That's why I write books like this, to show just what doing that looks like.

The pack of rescue dogs rushed me as I walked past the other casitas toward my car on the way to the gate. I like dogs, even if being in packs is not always my favorite way to encounter them, but what I soon realized was that they were most fascinated by my shoes, a richly seasoned pair of New Balance trainers that must have carried the strong scent of my own dog, Brownie. Kicking the dust off them against a tire, I climbed into my Ford and pulled away. Nearer the paddock I passed a stretch of ground with three rows of silvery water bowls, one for each of the dogs. This place was home for many other critters besides Deborah Axton's horses.

My final thought as I drove out through the black iron gate was that she had possessed the sheer grit to survive a voyage that had brought many others down as she passed by on her own journey toward home.

CHAPTER FIFTEEN
CHIP SWAB & FEED THE HUNGRY

If I turn west out of our bluff-side compound here at the edge of the village of Atotonilco, I drive over a hillside covered with lavender and down to a back road that also leads south toward San Miguel. We call this the back way, and in late summer, when the Río Laja bridge is flooded (see Chapter Six), it's our only way to get to town and back home.

Close to town, at the southern edge of the village of Ciénaguita, about half a kilometer before the railway station, there's a tiny cluster of homes and businesses, one with a landmark mural of Our Lady of Guadalupe against a white wall, and on the back side of it stands the tall pale warehouse owned by an organization called Feed the Hungry San Miguel. On a Tuesday morning in April I pulled into their parking lot at eight-fifteen, but I wasn't there for breakfast. I was scheduled to meet Chip Swab, the man who schedules and oversees the thirty-three delivery vehicles that bring food out to the countryside, known here as the *campo*.

Inside, the warehouse offers at least 10,000 square

feet of storage and offices. A vehicle track runs through it between a pair of yellow lines on the polished concrete floor. Rows of open steel shelves are divided and labeled into forty-four sections, of which thirty-seven are schools and seven others are charities. The pickups and SUVs were creeping through that morning, each one stopping before one of the sections, loading fresh fruits and vegetables, boxes containing pre-measured bags of rice and beans and lentils, four and five liter jugs of yogurt, and a dozen other ingredients. The name on each shelf section was that of a school. Not all of them could be found right around the corner. All the drivers furnish their own gas.

One thing that struck me immediately was that behind the shelves were pallets of, for example, fifty-kilo sacks of rice or beans, or any of several other commodities. But each pallet held only identical packages of the same product. The food collected by each driver today had been packed yesterday in quantities specifically measured out for each school.

I turned to Chip Swab, my guide for this tour. "You're not collecting donations of food, are you? Two slices of quiche and a half loaf of bread from last night's dinner party are not what we're looking at here."

"Not at all, our donations are monetary, or of people's time. The food is purchased outright in wholesale quantities. Our budget for the food part of our program is about $50,000 a month. That does not include the kitchens we build on each of the school grounds."

What I also learned was that the Feed the Hungry program was designed to promote good nutrition, not just fill empty stomachs. Each meal offered to a student includes three choices, and the menu is rotated every three months. To carry this out consistently the plan needs large quantities of each item. The meals are served at breakfast five days a week. The students are all registered in the program and their individual needs assessed. While some may be overweight, others may suffer from malnutrition, or sometimes both. A dietitian weighs them and assesses the requirements of each one.

From my own experience, I realized I was looking at a smoothly functioning business model in every sense of the word. This was no casual hit-or-miss effort for distributing random donations of extra food, it was a carefully thought out and executed system for feeding a large number of school children in a healthful and efficient way. In their literature I had read that they fed 4,000 children every day school was in session. In this year they will serve more than 900,000 meals.

Chip Swab finished loading his SUV and we headed out to the Dolores Hidalgo highway going north. About fifteen kilometers up the road, not far below the exit to the Los Labradores community, we turned right on an unmarked minor offshoot. When we set up this excursion earlier Chip had given me some information about his own background.

Born in Washington, D.C. in 1949, his parents had split up before he was three years old. He first lived with his mother, who had a dietician's certificate, until he was fourteen. Then he moved in with his father and his new family in Alexandria, VA.

"I finished my high school there. We didn't have the resources to send me to college, so I joined the Marine Corps when I graduated that summer. It was just in time to get to Vietnam for the Tet Offensive in 1968."

Even only a kilometer off the highway the road began to deteriorate quickly. The surrounding terrain was mostly rough pasture and struggling hayfield. Chip lurched to the right to avoid a rock the size of a bowling ball. Other than that he appeared to take no special notice of it.

"I had signed up originally for three years, and I asked if there was any other duty the Marine Corps had that would allow for more travel. One of the recruiters said he could get me into embassy guard school. At the time that school was in Arlington, VA, which was back home, and I successfully completed that. My first assignment was La Paz, Bolivia." He smiled. "It was considered a hardship post because of the altitude. It's at 11,500 feet. For some people it is a real adjustment, although others are able to make it fairly easily. I had no problems after about the first week. The program runs for two years, and if you're assigned to a normal post like Paris or London, you stay for those two years. But if you have a hardship post like La Paz, at the end of a year you were able to look at what openings there were in other parts of the world. I had become pretty fluent in Spanish, and Mexico City had an opening, so I chose that in 1970. That's where I met my wife, and we got married in 1971. We've been married ever since. She has a large family here in México. That brings us to where we are now."

Where we were now was a snaky turn through a tiny village and then off to the left on a one-lane dirt road through the houses.

"This is La Palma," he said. "They don't have a school here."

"It's interesting that you were in Mexico City, and I know you ended up for most of your working life in the States. Then you came back to México. When you got back here were you tempted then to return to Mexico City? How did you pick San Miguel as a place to settle once you retired in the States?"

At the edge of the village we swung around a pair of dusty trees in the middle of the road. You're not allowed to cut down trees here, even if they show up in inconvenient places.

"Mexico City is a big metropolis with air pollution problems, and the traffic is unbelievable. My first choice would've been Spain. We had traveled there before they joined the European Union, but once they joined, it didn't make economic sense anymore. Anyway, I've always loved the colonial architecture here. We had come for a wedding in San Miguel back in 1974. That was my first introduction to what was at that time a little pueblo. You could park in front of the Parroquia and drive around the *jardín*. We spent a memorable day at the hot springs, so we knew a little about San Miguel. Then we returned for a visit ten years ago. We drove through Los Frailes (a neighborhood on the south edge of town developed in the late sixties) and saw some lots for sale. At that time my wife had never even thought about coming back to México. She loved where we lived in Virginia and we had a lot of close friends there.

"When we bought the two lots, I told her that we may never build on them, they're only an investment. That was the first step. Obviously San Miguel is a community with a lot of expats, and a lot of cultural activities. It's got a great climate."

"Then were you both in agreement about coming back down here? Did you have to persuade her a little?"

"I did, and her family had to chip in on it too. The final decision was made easier by the fact that her mother was still alive then. She just passed away two years ago at the age of ninety-six. Lucy had a great relationship with her and her other siblings. She gave up her reservations and she's happy she's here now."

We were back on the road by then and the surface of it had deteriorated further. About thirty kilometers per hour was about as much as we could handle.

"This area has more than a hundred charitable organizations. What made you pick Feed the Hungry?" I tried not to look at the road as I said this, keeping a firm grasp on the hand grip over the door.

"A friend of mine named Will introduced me to it. I had heard of it but I wasn't sure exactly what they did. He was the driver coordinator, the job I have now. He asked me to become his assistant. If you don't have anybody to fill in for you during the school year it's hard to get away. That's how he introduced me to the whole process."

"What are we going to do today? Tell me about our destination."

"Today at the first school where we're going to deliver food I'll be filling in for a driver who is out of town. This place is called Las Cañas."

Chip drives a two year old Toyota Highlander and I suspected the farther in we got we'd be glad to have a vehicle with its high ground clearance and four wheel drive.

"The school at Las Cañas has about eighty kids. The delivery we make every Tuesday is the food that is consumed Monday through Friday in each of the schools. They have kitchens and cooks that are trained by our Feed the Hungry staff. The head chef at Feed the Hungry was fed as a child by this same program years ago. He grew up, got his education, and now he develops all the menus and holds the classes for the cooks. Most of the cooks are the mothers of kids that are in the schools."

My immediate thought was that Feed the Hungry also supplies a small regular payroll to women in these tiny towns, an asset that might otherwise be hard to find.

"Today we're going to deliver to Las Cañas first, and then go further out to La Palmilla, a much smaller school. It only has about forty kids there so there's not as much food. But as you will see, it's an even more challenging route to get there."

"How do you choose the schools that will be part of this program?"

"Most of the time they approach Feed the Hungry. A lot of these schools don't have a food program at all, so they don't serve any meals. Mostly what happens is that some of the mothers will get together and fill a wheelbarrow full of junk food. They come by the school during class sessions and the principal will let the kids come to the gate and buy that stuff, which is what they eat during the day. So when there's a need they either contact us through the State of Guanajuato government or through our staff and ask for us to consider adopting their school."

"What is the cost of that to them if you do agree to add them to your list?"

"Nothing."

"Nothing at all."

"If they have the land available we prefer to build a stand alone kitchen away from the school proper. There are other times when there's a suitable space within the school that can be converted to a kitchen. For us, that's a less expensive process. If it's available we'll use the existing space. We have a program called the Kitchen Angels where people make donations that are targeted to fitting out kitchens, like either doing the construction, or providing the appliances, the shelving, and washing facilities. That's how the kitchens usually get funded. Normally it takes several months to get it ready. Then we go out as a group and do an opening party. The community will prepare its own food, the mothers will come out, and the kids will do dances and sing. It's a big celebration."

"The sense I had immediately about Feed the Hungry, even as I came into the warehouse building, was the cleanliness, the layout, and the whole organization. It's that it is run like a serious for profit business. Scheduling is critical; it's like having a restaurant with three and a half dozen locations. Timing matters. The supply chain is critical. The staff is vital. Do you feel that your experience running an electrical contractor business in the States is a good fit for this?"

"Oh, absolutely. Any serious construction is all about schedules too. And it's all about being in the right place at the right time. The electrical contractor is almost never on what's called the 'critical path' of a new building. You have to put the foundation in, so the concrete has to be poured at a certain time. The steel structure has to be erected. What we did then didn't drive the overall project. Being able to come in and out according to their schedule, and have things on the site on time, was absolutely critical. The movement of material, the tools you'll need, and the manpower are the primary job."

"With your background in Latin America, both as an Embassy guard in Bogotá and Mexico City, and having married into a Mexican family, you seem like a natural to be running this part of the program. But where does all the food come from? Are the principal donations monetary or in supplies?"

"The principal donations are monetary. The problem is we're working from a fixed menu at each of the schools, and so the ingredient list becomes an important part of that. If you try to introduce donated food into that process, it just makes it that much harder to run it in an organized way. All the food purchases are done by the staff back at the warehouse. Olivia has been our program director for twenty-five years. She takes care of coordinating the other staff. They buy the dry goods in bulk because that way it's much cheaper. And then we have an outstanding fresh produce provider from Queré-taro that comes every Monday, having been told what our needs are. He makes a delivery of very high qual-ity fresh fruits and vegetables. They're packed on Mon-day and all of our drivers come in on Tuesday morning between seven-thirty and eight-thirty, as you saw before we left. They make the deliveries to forty-two separate sites."

We drove on for a while. I was wondering how much of this terrain had ever appeared on any map ever contemplated.

"Would it be accurate to say this is one of the more rewarding things you've ever done?" I hoped he didn't think I was talking about just getting there.

"Absolutely. We're coming now into Las Cañas, and you'll see how the little boys get very excited about the fact that the food has arrived. They keep the school grounds locked, but there's a bell at the gate. When they hear me ring it they know the food is out front. Each one wants to show you how strong he is and they help each other carry the food into the kitchen."

On the highest part of the town a ruined stone chapel from the colonial era sat next to a granary still partly intact. Most of the houses were constructed from haphazard materials, stone, stucco, red brick and concrete, one paycheck at a time. It can take a generation to build a house.

"We opened a new kitchen yesterday morning. There were sixty-six kids in that school. There was a little girl, a first grader, who was the first child in line. Her food was served and put on her tray and as she walked over to her table the smile on her face was priceless. She was so happy! In many cases the food they get in this program is the best that they eat all day. It introduces the mothers and the whole community to ingredients they have never used. They see eggplant and mushrooms, things they don't normally have access to out here. Part of it is an educational process, and that gets spread around to the rest of the community."

We pulled up before a pair of tall steel gates set in a long fence.

Just as he said, when Chip rang the bell there was a distant whoop of triumph from inside and a gang of elementary school boys piled up on the other side of the gate. Chip lifted the hatch at the back as the gate swung open.

"If a person reading this book wanted to get involved with Feed the Hungry," I said as the kids rushed toward us, "how would he or she go about that? Are you actively looking for people?"

He looked at me as the kids swarmed past him to attack the back of Toyota.

"Always. The San Miguel community is a real mix of people, some of whom live here part time. Most of the Canadians come down for the winter. In order to keep their health care plan active they have to go back home within six months. Other people that live here also have a home back in the States, so the turnover is constant. We have the packers who have to measure everything that goes out. The dry goods are packed on Saturday. There's a crew on Monday that packs all the fresh vegetables and fruits. Then we have the drivers on Tuesday. Typically in a week I'll have six or eight substitute drivers that I need to find because the regular driver is out of town, or there's a health issue. Some will have people visiting and can't make their school trip that week."

"Coming along might be instructive for the guests, though, wouldn't it? It's been instructive for me, and I live here."

"Right. So the opportunity to volunteer is almost limitless. Very seldom if you called us would you be told we have all the volunteers we can handle. We'll put you to work doing something."

"What would engage you here, Chip, if you weren't doing this?"

He looked away from the back of the SUV for a moment. "Well, you're probably going to get involved with something here, depending on what your interests are. If you're into music, there is a real live music scene here, guest artists that come for concerts. The theaters are very active. There's Casita Linda that goes out and builds homes for people that don't have one. There are many ways to get involved. I know very few people who live in this community that are not involved in some way. It's a limitless opportunity."

"It sounds like, during your years of being in business in the States, you were almost waiting to get back to Mexico."

"That is true. I was fortunate to be able to retire at the age of sixty-two, seven years ago. I had been given a chance to buy part of the company, so I was part owner. I notified everybody well in advance that on July first I was going to vacate the office I currently had and I was going to start enjoying the other parts of my life."

"You were president of the firm."

"Yes, I was, and I had been their first employee when they went into business in 1972. I was always in my office by seven in the morning and I seldom left before six or seven in the evening. It was a demanding process and there are other things you want to do in life. Coming back here was our goal and we spent eighteen months having a home built while we were still in the States. We were fortunate to find a great architect who designed exactly what we wanted. We have a second lot next to our house that's a garden and it has developed into a wonderful area. We thoroughly enjoy that part of our lives also."

"Would you say that this has become more like home than the U.S. was?"

"Yes, this is our home. I don't own any other property in the U.S. anymore. My son lives in northern Virginia. We're obviously happy to go back and visit with him and with great friends that still live in that area, but this is our home. I don't go back to the States for health care. I haven't signed up for Medicaid or Medicare. I could have veteran's benefits if I wanted them, but the health care I've experienced here in México is world class. There's no need. The cost is much lower; I can get the same medications for cholesterol and high blood pressure for much less, and it's the same prescription. This is home. It's where we'll be until we're not here anymore."

"To finish this up, although I know we could go on, what would you tell people who are looking for an organization like Feed the Hungry to join?"

"There are lots of organizations in San Miguel. If you have educational or work experience in certain areas, then there may be other organization where you might be a better fit. Not everybody would want to volunteer as a driver for us, for example. Some people here don't have their own vehicles. That doesn't preclude them from getting involved in terms of packing groceries for our deliveries. Here there are a number of locations, Soluciónes and la Conexión (both services that bring mail and packages down from the States), places that have information about all the different opportunities to get involved with charities that are doing this kind of work. Almost certainly once you get to know some of your neighbors you're going to find that they're involved in something, and they're going to ask you to come and see what they're doing, or to donate to the cause. Feed the Hungry has a very good website and that's where a lot of people make their first connection."

"Is joining an organization like this also a good way to meet people?"

"Absolutely! What I really enjoy about San Miguel is the diversity of the people we meet here, from all walks of life. In most cases, people do not end up here who are not well traveled. They've already been to other places trying to decide where to retire. San Miguel has some kind of strange atmosphere that means that people can come down for a one week vacation and go back home having bought a house here. It's the kind of thing that hits them within the first twenty-four or forty-eight hours. But the diversity of the people is what makes life here so full. You meet a lot of interesting people."

"Let's wrap it up right there, Chip. I think we've just proven that."

On the way back to town we talked about politics, American and Mexican, and about how good it was to be slightly removed from both. We pulled back into the warehouse parking lot just when he said we would. It reminded me of scheduling and commitments, and how pragmatic this business was. We had never gotten into the origin of Feed the Hungry, other than to say it had been around since 1984, but the structure of it now was clearly the work of some experienced and businesslike minds. To operate on that scale, to be the master of its mission, it absolutely had to be that way.

Tax-deductible donations can be made through Feed the Hungry San Miguel, Inc. (US) or Amistad Canada.

CHAPTER SIXTEEN
HEATHER HANLEY

It was a Thursday morning in the week after Easter when I went into the *el centro* district to have a conversation with Heather Hanley. I had known her for a number of years and what I liked about her background was that she had come here alone and managed her life in a way that totally suited her needs.

It felt like a warm day coming, but at nine-fifteen, the car traffic wasn't troublesome yet. Like the one before it, that week is still a school holiday here, so a lot of the Mexican nationals from other parts of the country hadn't left town yet. When local people talk about tourism in San Miguel, it still refers mostly to other Mexicans. This is the town where independence from Spain was declared in 1810. Eleven years later, Spain finally agreed when the commander of their military forces changed sides.

By this time of the year, many of the American and Canadian snowbirds have gone home or are about to, and the Floridians and Texans fleeing the heat have not yet arrived. It's a lull in traffic to some degree.

Heather Hanley lives on Mesones, the old street of inns and hospices for weary travelers of earlier centuries, a time when travel was difficult, dangerous and expensive. Her building, now divided into condos, was once apparently part of a school. On the far corner up at Hidalgo is an active convent, and at the other end on Hernandez Macias is the old church called Las Monjas, The Nuns (see the cover of this book). The Bellas Artes, closer to Heather's corner, was also once a large convent and serves as a cultural center today.

Parking cars was understandably not on anyone's town planning agenda in 1700, so my choices were limited. In *el centro* it's the kind of motoring climate where if you spot a parking place as you drive by you feel you need to take it out of principle, even if you're not headed anywhere in that area. To ignore that kind of luck would be imprudent. Once in place at the curb you can sit behind the wheel and congratulate yourself for having done something nearly impossible, even if also nearly meaningless.

I ended up in a "ramp" on Insurgentes near the Biblioteca, two blocks from Heather's building. This structure is as clear an example of the Mexican workaround as you could ever encounter. Despite its compete inappropriateness, a three-story building was gutted and restructured inside to improvise a parking venue. Driving into the near total darkness inside (turn your lights on as you enter), the main floor spaces are all roped off for people with more clout than you will ever acquire in ten lifetimes. Just to illustrate this level of privilege, they are mostly empty. The only other choice going forward is a slope set at an alarming angle that may be too much of a challenge for your aging car, ribbed with concrete as if to accommodate tanks on a field exercise in Flanders in 1916, and with no thought of side rails. The angle of ascent is so steep you cannot see beyond the nose of your car other than a narrow glimpse of the ceiling, which is much too close. Once you level off you need to take an immediate hairpin turn to the left to avoid hitting a column and a parked car, a fact you do not discover until you have leveled off. By then you can no longer maneuver into that turn without backing a few feet down again at an alarming angle that could rip up the underside of your car. It illustrates why Mexicans believe so firmly in fate. Nothing else is ever going to save them.

All the designated spaces are designed for nothing larger than a Mini Cooper or a Fiat 500. Contrary to the dizzy core beliefs of the people who planned this, just painting yellow lines on the floor doesn't make a parking place, at least not for people who had planned to exit their cars. They are sandwiched in pairs between concrete columns that bear the scars of many close encounters of the parking kind. Here any kind of crew cab pickup is a bad dream. The acrid reek of claustrophobia and frustration hangs heavily upon the air at any time of day.

Coming downward on the way out, the floor at the base level of the ramp is deeply scarred by the impact of the crumpled noses of previous parking customers imprudently but understandably in a rush to escape their accelerating sense of claustrophobia. You can also spot them here and there on the street, cars that look like they have spent much of their useful lives driving up and down stairways in total darkness.

But by then I was on foot and soon I emerged into the daylight traffic of Calle Insurgentes. It was time to repair my mood.

Rehearsing a cheerful grin on the dull screen of my cell phone, I actively reengineered my attitude as I approached Heather's house. While this area is definitely 'Old México,' the ramp is one of those small pockets within it that belong to nowhere you'd want to go. In any case, these expat conversations are never about me, and writing a book is a task that always brings its innate challenges.

In her building down on Mesones not far from the Angela Peralta Theater, a keypad offered me a range of choices. I found the right one and Heather Hanley buzzed me in.

The courtyard inside was faced mostly with roughly fitted stone, with numerous windows and several stairways, a space of great character and of indeterminate age. It could easily have undergone several reincarnations. That's not unusual. Our main library had once been a convent and later, a slaughterhouse. Even as I pushed the door closed I felt the silence settle over me. It was instantly an inviting place, apart from whatever might be going on out in the street.

Upon entering Heather Hanley's apartment on the second floor I was instantly struck by how very far from a workaround it was. While it was crowded with furniture and art, it was at the same time comfortable and inviting. With two sofas set at a right angle, the fireplace projected a sculptural presence into the living room.

She is a woman of medium height and polished appearance. At seventy-eight years old she does not appear to have slowed down discernably, and her delivery as we talked was thoughtful and articulate. Even if I didn't know her I would guess that she had spent a lot of time in commerce, in one on one situations, because she has the kind of poise that comes from long experience in business.

After a chat off the record, we sat at her dining table and I drank a V8 for this discussion.

"Heather, I know from our earlier conversations that you've lived in several other parts of the world. Can you tell me a bit about some of those places? Did any of them seem like home at the time?"

"Well, most of them did. When I was a child we moved a great deal, since my father was in the Army Air Corps, which became the Air Force in 1947. My mother and father were always under the same roof with my younger sister and me, and that was always home when I was growing up. Then, much later when I graduated from college and decided I wanted to live in Italy because it was so beautiful, and I spoke Italian and loved it, it was just wherever I happened to be that I made my own family. I spent a lot of time alone. I had a roommate that first year, but after that I lived by myself."

"Given those experiences, I find it interesting that you chose to settle in this town of San Miguel, and in this country of México. You must've had many other options to consider. I can see that you've made yourself quite comfortable here, so I don't think the cost of living was the driving concern. How long have you been here and what brought you to earth in San Miguel?"

"I've been here full time since the summer of 2004. I visited the first time in the summer of 2003 because at the end of 2002 my husband died and I was very much at loose ends. It was an unexpected death, even though he was almost ninety. Because I had spent cumulatively thirty-four years of my life in Italy, spoke Italian and was familiar with the culture, I had at first thought I would go back and live there full time. I asked a friend living in Italy to find me a rental for hurricane season, because at the time we'd been living in a condo we owned in South Florida, north of Miami and south of Fort Lauderdale, in a little municipality called Sunny Isles Beach."

"In those circumstances, Italy must've looked like a comforting option."

"But my friend said to me, 'Don't go back to Italy now. You have too many memories of him there. Go someplace where you never spent any time with him at all. Because you speak Italian and French, go down to San Miguel de Allende and study Spanish. It's a beautiful town and I think you'll like it.'

"So I came down here that first summer and I was enchanted, as many people are. I found it was a very open town. It was tolerant, and I felt I was welcomed, even though in the United Sates many people had considered me very odd, having lived so much time abroad as I had, and been comfortable with it. I just feel freer and more relaxed here. I've noticed it is very easy to meet people in San Miguel and I have always felt welcome."

"Were costs any concern at that time?"

"Not really, although when it comes to the financial side of things, Italy is at least twice as expensive as San Miguel. I would've had to have a car, and then there are the big, as I discovered after I came to live here, difficulties of living in Italy full time. The Schengen countries do not make it easy for you. You can be there for ninety days then you have to be away for ninety days."

"How unsettling! What was that word? I don't think I know it."

"Schengen, and it's capitalized."

"I've never heard of it."

"It's a European Union agreement that relates to border and passport issues. A lot of these countries have joined it because they don't want to be flooded with immigrants. I realized that what I loved so much about Italy in the early sixties, when I lived there, was what I found here. Mexicans are more open to foreigners than even the Italians were then. And Italians do like foreigners. They're not at all a xenophobic culture. The Mexicans here made me welcome, and then there was so much to do. I had inadvisedly enrolled in Level Four of a local Spanish language school without ever having studied any Spanish."

"That was very nervy of you."

"Well, I knew I could bluff my way through, and I've never been afraid to try to express myself. I have no shame. I know I'm going to make mistakes, but I knew I could communicate."

"I won't ask how that went, but there are many grades of Spanish proficiency here, often starting with zero. If you were out of control you would not stand out that much. What does stand out for me so many years later is that you have stayed and found a place for yourself here. That connects to one of the questions I have for myself and one that is driving this book, among others. Where is home? And if San Miguel has truly become home for you, what does that mean, bottom line?"

I drained my V8 as she considered this.

"In a basic sense, home is where you want to go after traveling. Home is where you feel most comfortably at ease and most of your friends reside or come to stay. That's definitely the case for me with San Miguel. There was a fellow here named Will whom I was once seated next to at a dinner party. He said that he evaluated each place he was considering for retirement with the test of four Cs: cost, culture, community, and climate. He felt San Miguel blew everything else out of the water. I wish I could say I had thought of that, but it was his finding. Anyway, it's home because my friends are here. It's home because I was fortunate enough to find a really beautiful apartment that I love to live in, and I was able to bring my things out of storage. It's home because I speak Spanish, I read Spanish, and I can write it, not as well. But I have a lot of Mexican friends, with whom I can speak Spanish, and I think that's such an important part of being in the culture. In fact, when I go back to Italy I think I'm speaking Italian, but they're so close that I often get them confused."

"Possibly because many of us are of a certain age, numerous expat residents of San Miguel are single women. Some came down here on their own, and many others were widowed here if they arrived as part of a couple. Is that a good situation for them, to be living by themselves in Mexico? They must not be listening to the American press or the State Department."

"The reason it is a good situation is because as you grow up your family are your blood relatives. Later, when you go out into the world you may still think of your family as your blood relatives, but that is not always the case. It certainly isn't the case for me, because I am widowed and I am orphaned. I never had children and I am estranged from my only sibling, although I have a very close relationship with her older daughter, who also is estranged from her mother."

"Families can be a kind of crucible for many people. I can testify to this, but you have the floor on that issue."

She gave me a broad grin. "And so, in San Miguel, I find that the people who come down here are well educated, the ones of retirement age that I know, and well traveled, pretty sophisticated, open minded, and they think outside of the box. So with eight other women, we have a support group we call our Health Group. We meet the first Monday of every month at a restaurant and we discuss health issues. For example, I've found out some very interesting things about advanced health care directives from one of the other members."

"These are the instructions you would leave for what care you would wish to have toward the end of your life, and what you would prefer to avoid, should you be unable to articulate them at that time."

"Exactly, and we have each others' emergency contact information. In many cases we have house keys. We check in with each other. We socialize, but we also look out for each other."

"The very definition of support. Are you a member of the Twenty-four Hour Association?"

"Absolutely! I cannot say enough good things about it! I think it is a splendid organization. The people that run it should be canonized. They really make it work for us, because Mexican bureaucracy is horrible."

"Anyone who has read this book this far has seen my detailed chapter on it."

"Wonderful!"

"Was there a particular time or moment when you first realized that San Miguel de Allende was going to be your home?"

"It was during my first summer living in this apartment, in 2004. I was walking up to the main covered market, Ignacio Ramirez, to buy some flowers. You go up past the Plaza Civica, and the morning is coming at you as you're walking east. There was a little girl and somebody had given her a bubble wand. She was making huge floating bubbles. They were huge, the size of your head, and they were iridescent and beautiful. I was looking at them and I thought, 'I am happy here because San Miguel has given me a bubble of intelligence, creativity and business, and when you look at the number of philanthropic organizations or NGOs, a bubble of good intentions. And if this isn't the real world, I don't care. I'm happy here."

"I have written about reality as it's presently constituted, and it's not my favorite option either. Fortunately we have other choices. We can be readers and writers of fiction. But that's a different story. You must've witnessed a lot of changes in San Miguel during your time here. Has it gotten better, or not? Some people who've been here for a while have told me they feel the door should be closed to anyone else coming in after them. I never responded to it in that way, but hearing it announced like that, I sometimes felt that earlier residents might've equally said that to them as they appeared at the gate, visas in hand. Were they just pulling rank or seniority?"

"Well, I also disagree completely with that attitude. What keeps San Miguel so wonderful is the new blood that keeps coming in. The older people are all going to die. We all hope God is going to make an exception in our case, but I don't think so. Anyway, that's what keeps it so vibrant and interesting. It's such a strong creative community, and creative people are, I think by their nature, open to the world. That's what makes it so wonderful. I think San Miguel has gotten much, much better. We have more theaters, lectures, concerts, and dozens of new international restaurants. I'm very near the Angela Peralta Theater down at the corner, where there is something going on most of the time. I would be silly if I wasn't going to it, because if I don't like the program that night I can just come home again.

"Then there's the business of traffic, which is what most people complain about. I never brought a car down here and I never wanted to drive in México, although earlier in my life I happily drove across the United States, up into Canada, and all over Europe and into Morocco in North Africa. Inexpensive taxis are plentiful here in the center and I have the telephone numbers of several radio taxi companies. I do hope the city council comes up with a solution to traffic. There is one that has been in place for years in hundreds of small, historic UNESCO World Heritage towns. The way it works is that you make people park on the edges of town and give them free electric buses or shuttles to get to the center. It's a solvable problem that's been done everywhere."

"Given the antagonistic posture of the current U.S. administration toward México, have you ever experienced any hostile response on this end from Mexicans?"

Heather brushed this idea away. "No, I have not. That could be because the Mexicans that I know, the ones that are my friends are just as appalled by the leadership in the United States, if you can call it that, and we sympathize with each other."

"Living in the *el centro* district makes it easy to get around without a car, but are there times when you find it has too much going on?"

This was nothing new to her. "Of course. There are times when if I go out my front door, because I'm on Mesones, sometimes there's a parade marching up the street, and it's hard to make my way. But most of the time you can learn very quickly which days those are going to be. I am fortunate that one of my favorite restaurants nearby will deliver food to me. They're right around the corner. But I'm perfectly happy on my own here, if it gets difficult out there."

"And as we sit here," I said, craning my neck back toward the front windows, "I can't hear a single sound from the street, even though we are right downtown."

"No, the walls are this thick." Smiling, she extended her arms to indicate a meter or more.

"What things keep you busy here?"

"Well, my primary volunteer activity is helping Pro Musica. I started this about nine years ago with Michael Pearl, who heads that group. I'm working on the dinners and cocktail parties, the reservations and the cancellations. It's a data base job that starts in August and goes through March. Beyond that, there are, as I mentioned, many activities at the Angela Peralta, the PEN lectures at the Bellas Artes, the plays and movies at the Santa Ana, and we have two little art cinemas in town. I also like to read, and I generally read about three hours a day, because I love it. I consider it a great luxury. Even though our library here doesn't have enough titles to accommodate me, Kindle has saved my life. I have more than 1,400 titles on my Kindle. Those are the ones I've read, mostly."

"I find that living full time beyond the U.S. border gives me a different perspective on what goes on up there. Does it work that way for you, and how do you feel about the U.S. now after your long time in San Miguel?"

Her tone remained upbeat, even as a frown creased her forehead. "I still think it's a great country, although I believe it's being led very badly right now. I just shudder when I think what's being done with the revolving door cabinet, with the sort of tin pot tyrant who's at the head of all that. I would be just as aware of this in the United States, but I would be even more distressed by it there. As we know, stress kills, and one of the things people do by living down here in San Miguel is to lower their level of stress. One of the great freedoms I have besides being able to read three hours a day is never having to spend time with people I don't like. I am very fortunate that way. If there is someone I don't like I can find a way to minimize contact, but that almost never happens now."

"Some people who have read my other expat books about México have commented that they read like a conversation. I hope that's true for most readers, because I think that kind of intimacy on the page is important. If this interview is your conversation with people thinking about living in México, and how they would do that, what would you say to them that they might not read somewhere else?"

Heather's slow nod suggested that she had thought this one out earlier. As with everyone I talked to for this book, I had sent her the questions in advance, so that there would be time to consider any that required more forethought.

"I think the first thing you need to do is figure out where you're going to live in San Miguel. There are many different neighborhoods. Some people will come back for several years at a stretch to spend a month or two or three, and will intentionally pick different neighborhoods to try them out. I knew immediately that I wanted to live in *el centro*, so it wasn't an issue for me. And the other thing, at least as important if not more, is to study Spanish. I know that's not easy for everybody, and I know that aging gringo brains don't pick up new information as quickly as they once did. I was fortunate because I already had a leg up that way. But if you speak Spanish—México is basically a country that runs on courtesy when it comes to social interactions. The courtesy you show local people by speaking their language is something they always appreciate."

We said our thanks and goodbyes.

As I stepped back onto the sidewalk on the ancient Calle Mesones, as old as any part of this sixteenth century town, my sense of the conversation was that each of the places Heather Hanley had lived, starting even as a small child, had prepared her exquisitely to live in San Miguel. If there had been issues she didn't bring up, they apparently had not lasted and she had come to earth here in a most relaxed and satisfying fashion.

Perhaps "coming to earth" would be my new definition of home. But I knew that other conversations were coming, other points of view. I had known Heather for years without asking these questions. I liked her firm handle on things, her concrete engagement. I walked back up Mesones knowing that this chapter would be a good one.

CHAPTER SEVENTEEN
JOHN AND LAURA BLY

On a Sunday afternoon late in April I was fortunate enough to find a parking place on Calle Quebrada behind the Hotel Sautto. April and May are the hottest months in San Miguel, before the rainy spells of June through September moderate the weather. After a chilly winter the heat felt welcome.

Quebrada is a street I always enjoy walking from beginning to end because that's where my fictional detective, Paul Zacher, has lived over the course of twenty-two mysteries. The challenge has always been to identify which house is his, although I have never been able to. None of them looks quite the way it does in my imagination or in the books, and reality always takes second place to fiction, as it should.

The two and three story façades, built flush with the narrow sidewalks, display a variety of finishes and styles. This narrow street usually carries little traffic. Parking runs from chancy to nonexistent. I have been invited to parties at a couple of these properties, and at least two of the narrow fronts mask startling estates behind, although most are ordinary houses.

On one of very few side streets I found the home of John and Laura Bly. The timing was fortunate, since they had quite recently returned from an extended jaunt in the Far East, and John was soon to leave for another in the States. I wanted to catch them together. They are, perhaps more than any others that I know, a couple in motion. I wondered whether that implied a different meaning in terms of how they defined home. Were they searching for it, or had they either given up on it or redefined the term? Did they care about home at all? Perhaps the question does not even look the same to them as to some other people I've talked to for this book.

The Blys had been present at a dinner party in our previous house in town where the question of home and its various meanings first came up. That conversation provided a question that still hung in the air and was the seed that developed into this book, so they were an ideal pair with whom to take it up again somewhat later. We had all certainly had much more time to think about it. The answers I'd received so far in these conversations were so diverse I was already wondering whether any general conclusion would be possible, not that I'm inclined to generalize.

When I examine this question for myself I always think of what I require in terms of consistency and calm in order to write an average of two and a half books a year. Although it works for some people to have two homes, one in the U.S. and one here, it is an option my wife and I have always rejected. We most emphatically did not want to be running back and forth across the border.

In contrast, the Blys run back and forth between their San Miguel house and a wide variety of other venues. They rarely have much of their stuff around them. This is another reason why I thought they'd be a natural choice for this discussion, which I suspect that despite the input of an number of well informed and insightful people, will end with no consistent and predictable definition of home. But that's a larger story, and even as I write this closer to the end of the book, I have to confess that I don't know how it ends.

Although it was a bright afternoon, as most are, I stood in deep shadow within the narrow *callejón* (literally, alley) and rang their bell. The Blys are in their sixties, each of them active and trim. If they are both retired from their former businesses, John as a consultant for the one of the large U.S. accounting firms, and Laura as a travel writer for *USA Today*, their manner does not suggest they have retired from anything else that might engage them. The sense of ongoing exploration is palpable in speaking with both of them.

We went inside and chatted for a while in a small inner courtyard. Their principal outdoor space is on the roof, called here the *azotea*. I had a sense that we were coming back together on this topic after a long pause. This is not the first book of mine that was conceptually launched at that dinner table, and when we moved to the country a year ago, it was a priority that it come with us.

"I guess we need to start some with some kind of background," I said, "so let's begin with what each of you did in your past life and how you came to settle in San Miguel."

"We met in Chicago," Laura began, "right out of college at what was aptly named International Village. It was a swinging singles apartment complex near the O'Hare Airport. I was in Heidelberg, and John was in Zurich in faux European-themed apartment buildings."

"Swinging singles wasn't really what they were," John said, his eyebrows lifting slightly.

"Well, there were a lot of pilots and flight attendants, and people like us just starting off in their careers. And there were no children allowed. You couldn't do that now," Laura continued. "After we got married and moved to Los Angeles, I continued in newspaper journalism, this time as a travel writer and editor, and John continued his consulting. We both traveled extensively, but he had a very different travel mode and experience than I did. I'd be off to Mendocino for the weekend, or Hawaii for the week."

"And I," John added, "was traveling almost every

week, but staying in hotels and working up to eighteen hours a day. Sometimes Laura was able to finagle an assignment in the city where I was based, so we'd meet in Phoenix or Dallas and she'd do a story. Travel has always been part of our relationship together."

"So being on the road was the basic pattern early on. How did San Miguel come to be part of that process?"

Laura poured us a glass of wine. "I first visited here on a travel assignment, when I came down to do a story tied to the town's 450th anniversary in 1992. I remember interviewing Stirling Dickinson (San Miguel's first expat American artist, and a founder of the Instituto Allende) in his orchid garden, listening to his story about seeing those fanciful spires of La Parroquia for the first time and deciding right then and there to stay. And, in the back of my mind, I thought that this could be a creative, inspiring place to retire."

"But at the time," added John, "you weren't infatuated with México, either before you left or even after you got back."

"No, I wasn't. I hadn't done a lot of traveling here, and I equated it with drunk college kids in Tijuana or overcrowded Cancún beaches, and I'm not a beach person. One story I had done in the mid-eighties was on the town of Loreto in Baja California. They were starting a new tourist development and promoting it as 'the next Cancún.' They had advertisements in L.A. saying, 'where the mountains meet the sea,' and showing these gorgeous white sand beaches. I told my editor, 'Why don't we check this out? Is it really the next Cancún?'

"I went down and discovered early on that the white sand beaches were a choppy boat ride away on an island in the Sea of Cortez. The hotel electricity and water would go on and off, and I got sick from the food. And I thought, well, México is just not a place that draws me."

"So ironically, here we sit much later." My arm swept the room. "Did you leave a place behind in the States when you moved down here?"

"No," John said. "In late 2013, we had an offer to do a home exchange in San Miguel from a part time resident we'd met through a mutual friend who had taken a writing workshop here. I had already retired, and Laura had recently taken a buyout at *USA Today*. We knew we wanted to make a major lifestyle change, and the plan was to sell our house and belongings in Washington, D.C. to travel full-time. Spending a month in San Miguel seemed like a good way to test drive what we'd hoped would become a long-term adventure, living out of suitcases and getting to sample other cultures in other people's homes."

Here Laura paused with a thoughtful look.

"So there was a problem?" I said.

She nodded with an ironic expression. "At the end of the month, we weren't ready to go back to D.C. It was December, and the *posadas* (nightly reenactments of Mary and Joseph's search for a room in Bethlehem) were in full swing. We were invited into neighbors' homes for *ponche* (Christmas punch), and we kept contrasting the warm, un-commercial atmosphere with the frenzied buying push back in the States. Meanwhile, we'd met some new friends who had a rental place on Loreto and they said, 'Do you want to stay another couple of weeks?' So our month turned into six weeks.

"The following summer we sold the house, packed our rolling duffels, and hit the road on an extended driving trip to visit family in New England and the Midwest. But we kept thinking about San Miguel, and came back that fall for a rental that turned into three months. The year after that, we rented for five months. And then we decided, what the hell." She made a gesture of surrender with both hands.

"At first, we'd returned thinking that this was still a temporary landing spot, but we developed some great friendships and those drew us back as much as the place itself. We made the decision early on that we were going to cut our U.S. ties completely, and traveling will always be a major focus in our lives. But buying a home in San Miguel as a refuge and a base for exploring just made sense."

"Our place is the world," John said. "In a way, we didn't leave anything behind. We shared the world with San Miguel and that's what we're doing now." He has a soft-spoken manner that even with his interest in facts, is occasionally tinged with irony.

"You sold your house virtually turnkey," I said. "You walked away with your suitcases. What was that like?"

"It was liberating," Laura said. "We had decorated our house in an eclectic, contemporary style with purchases from our previous travels, and the couple who bought it were moving from a typical suburban home. After we accepted their offer, the wife came back to look at buying our patio furniture and we started chatting. I was telling her, 'we bought that rug in Iran, and that painting above the fireplace was from Ecuador, and that wall hanging was from Guatemala.' Everything had a story behind it, and at the end of what had become a long visit, she turned to me and said, 'I know you're going to think this is crazy, but you're changing your life and we want to change ours. I love your house, and I love everything in it. We want to buy it lock, stock, and barrel.' It really seemed that the universe was validating our decision.

"On our last night in the house, we loaded our car and it looked like a scene from the Clampetts in *The Beverley Hillbillies* or the Joads in *The Grapes of Wrath*. But the new owners had bought almost all our furnishings, and when we walked out for the last time, the sheets were on the bed, the dishes were in the cupboards."

"What interests me in that context is that you've come into a similar condition here," I said. "Was this house an estate situation?"

"The husband had died," John said, "and the wife had decided to move back to the States. As in many situations like that, she sold the whole thing."

We were all silent for a moment before I spoke again. "That leads to where this has been going in my mind with some of the other narratives in this book. Some people, in trying to define the meaning of home for themselves, have said home is where their stuff is. That leads me to ask, What is your attachment to your 'stuff'? Apparently that is not the way you define home."

They answered in unison. "No."

"Whenever we were home for more than a few weeks, Laura would start to get itchy feet," John said, "so spending money on travel was more important to us than buying new cars and furniture."

"Your interest in meditation must have been helpful in keeping your focus." We had spoken about this earlier.

"Well, my practice in Zen is a more spiritual practice. You are not your things; you are something else. You can live a better life that way. We have always wanted to be out in the world, and our attachment is to learning new things and meeting new people."

"Would you say that home is a place in your head? Does it even have a physical location?"

"Home is a sanctuary of comfort," John said, "and wherever we travel, we bring along things like portable Bose speakers so we can have our own music, and a folding plastic vase so we'll always have fresh flowers. But home is not necessarily a physical sanctuary."

"To go back to your question of whether home is in your head," Laura added, "a few years ago, before we got this house, I found a small *retablo* (shadow box) here in San Miguel that said '*Tu hogar es donde esta tu corazon.*' I knew when I bought it that it was compact enough to put in a suitcase, so I could put it up in whatever airbnb or hotel we were staying in. And it was a great reminder that home really is where your heart is."

"San Miguel was recently named again in a magazine survey as the best place in the world to live, or at least to visit. How does that relate to your view of it?"

"It's positive and negative," Laura said. "We used to live in a suburb of D.C. that is a tourist town in its own right. Some of our neighbors complained about the traffic, the tour buses, the noise from partiers filling up bars on the weekends. But we always felt that an influx of visitors was an advantage. There was a good choice of restaurants, a movie theater within walking distance, and lots of cultural activities. In many ways, tourism enhances and facilitates those things. But the flip side of that—are you familiar with the term UNESCOcide?"

"Yes," I said. "It happens when all the squawking vitality has been buffed out of a place to make it into a more static image that conforms to the rules of being a World Heritage Site."

Laura nodded. "Well, I worry that San Miguel is in danger of becoming a victim. We certainly saw evidence of that effect on our trip to Southeast Asia last winter. Luang Prabang in Laos and Hoi An in Vietnam are World Heritage cities, and they've both become overrun with tourists, they're almost stage sets."

"I noticed some of that when we returned to San Miguel, where a whole crop of hip new restaurants had opened while we were gone. Sometimes I feel that the historic centro is one shop after a restaurant after a hotel, and I cringe when I hear we're becoming 'the Hamptons of México.' We talked to a friend who lives down the street on Quebrada, and she said that during Semana Santa (Holy Week) this year, she was afraid that the bridge over Calle Canal would collapse under the weight of all the tourists taking selfies at sunset.

"But on the other hand, all I have to do is walk five minutes down to Mercado San Juan de Dios, where you can buy everything from cauliflower to cowboy boots. My favorite *florista* there knows me and what flowers I like. He encourages my stumbling Spanish and gives me free rose petals for my fountain. There is still a sense of local commerce, of local community that is flowing all around us and is welcoming us as *extranjeros* (strangers), which is amazing to me. They're not fed up with us, they still embrace us with a smile and with joy."

"Hearing you say that leads me to ask for a conclusion from that train of thought. Has this town then become home?"

"We weren't looking for a permanent home when we started out," said Laura, "and I'd always loved that disconnected but exhilarating feeling of waking up in a strange place and, for a few moments, not knowing where I was. In more than thirty years as a professional traveler, I'd never felt homesick - until we came here. The only place I've ever really missed is San Miguel."

"When you travel, do you like to revisit favorite places or do you usually go to ones you haven't been to before? Are you filling in the blanks?"

"Yes, I guess you could say that," said Laura. "It's a big world, and until San Miguel we've rarely wanted to return to destinations we've already visited. People tell me, 'you've been to seven continents and a hundred countries. You've been everywhere.' Well no, we're only getting started."

"Do you ever get sick on the road?"

"A bit," said John, "but I think we're getting

better at handling it. There's always Google translate, so no matter what the language you can communicate with a pharmacist."

"Last winter," added Laura, "we were at a resort in the middle of nowhere in northern Laos that offered climbing up to a waterfall and zip lining back down. I was alone on this zip line with a local guide who spoke no English, and I had this moment when I thought, 'if I fall and break an ankle, or worse, how long will it take to airlift me to Bangkok?' But travel is a leap into the unknown. And as an expat in San Miguel, it's a leap into comfort and a close sense of community."

"Going back to the learning theme," John said, "in San Miguel we're improving our Spanish and discovering more about Mexican culture and history. There's adult education, a lot of art and music events, and creative, interesting people. Being here is part of that whole spectrum of growing and learning."

"You mentioned Zen before. I was trying to research meditation for writing this chapter, and the first thing I found is that there is little agreement on what it is. What is it to you?"

"To me, meditation is a form of exercise for your mind, part of the growing process. When they've done brain scans of meditators, they've found that the areas of your mind that relate to anxiety shrink, so you become a calmer person. A better person to be around, a better person to travel with. So for me, meditation is a lifetime habit."

"What role does place play in meditation? I know that here you have a nearby meditation center, but how do you meditate on the road? Is it more difficult?"

"I love to meditate with a community, and it's great to go out and have a coffee afterwards. But the nice thing about meditation is that you can do it anywhere. I also have a Zen master who gives private interviews and a talk twice a week, which I join online. He's based in Korea but he leads retreats in different places, which now include San Miguel."

"Do you tend to make comparisons between the places you visit and San Miguel?"

"We do," Laura said. "On this most recent trip, we were in Southeast Asia for nearly three months. The night we got back to México, we flew into León and drove through the sunset, through that amazing high desert light. We arrived home about half an hour after the last of the afterglow. We poured a glass of champagne and walked straight up to the *azotea*, and realized we hadn't seen stars like that in a month or more because it had been cloudy and humid so much of the time. The weather here is pretty darn perfect. And as we were standing there, I suddenly saw a white shadow crossing the edge of my vision. It was a lone egret, shining in the light of a half moon. It was such an astonishing and miraculous moment, and I realized, once again, that those kind of moments happen all the time here."

"We joke that we've already made closer connections in San Miguel than we did in nearly twenty years in D.C. I think it's because we're all transplants," John said. "We're more open to new people and experiences. We were at dinner recently and discussing some of these issues, and one of our friends said that one of the things he appreciates most about San Miguel is that every day something surprises and delights him. That is so true for us as well."

"That is surely worth a lot," I said.

"It's incalculable," Laura said.

"There's always a lot of talk from the US government and the media about how dangerous México is. As people who spend a lot of time in other places, how true do you think that is, relative both to the U.S. and to other places you visit?"

"It's true that we travel to places many people probably wouldn't go. A picture of a memory popped up on my Facebook page, and there I was at the Egyptian Museum in Cairo, flashing a peace sign next to a grinning Egyptian soldier with a tank in the background. We were there three months after the revolution, and it was one of the best trips of our lives. And we were in Turkey two summers ago, after multiple bombings. We felt welcome, and never in danger."

"Most people," added John, "will paint a broad picture. We think it's important to look at the statistics of a place, and research the specifics that other people aren't discerning."

"And so the bottom line is..."

"We feel safe here. We're planning a trip to Morelia and Patzcuaro in Michoacán, which according to the U.S. State Department is a "no go" destination. We took a great tour to the Copper Canyon and Chihuahua a few years ago, where the State Department urges Americans to 'reconsider travel due to crime.'"

"Throughout Southeast Asia, one of the first questions anyone asked was, 'Where are you from?' To answer 'México' flummoxed everyone," said Laura. "In Vietnam, we took a motorcycle tour between Hoi An and Hue with two young women from Dusseldorf, Germany. When we told them where we lived they said, 'México? It's so dangerous!' And I thought, in Germany even? Then we had to go into the explanation, 'No, not really, unless you're involved in a cartel, or fuel theft, or you know someone who is. And anyone can be a victim of random violence...especially in the United States."

"Are you renting this house out when you travel?" I asked. "How is it to have other people living in your space?"

"We've been renting places around the world," said John, "and we're going to keep doing that indefinitely. The idea in purchasing here was not so much that we were buying a home for ourselves, but that we were buying a rental property we could live in, one that would be better than the properties we were getting before. We decided that in San Miguel in *el centro*, where we wanted to live and most tourists want to be staying, it made financial sense to buy and rent it out during the peak winter months."

"Part of it was that we didn't have an emotional investment to the stuff in this house," Laura said, "and if we'd been starting from scratch we would have made different design choices. So we have made some additions. Behind me is a photograph that I took from a window in one of our San Miguel rentals, which is the first time I've actually printed one of my photos and framed it. That brings me joy. But photos and fresh paint are small things, and I'm hoping we don't get sucked into making too many major changes. We've talked to people who say, 'I couldn't imagine some stranger sleeping in my bed.' But we've slept in so many different beds over the years. A bed is a bed, and I don't have any proprietary attachment to it."

"In the context of this conversation, what would you tell people who are looking at your lifestyle and considering whether they would ever fit into it?"

"One of the things I love about San Miguel," Laura added, "is its sense of transience. As well-traveled expats and tourists we may be here for various reasons, but most of us are passionate about the place. We come and go, and this is an ideal base for exploration because the town itself sparks inspiration, whether it's internal or external."

As I left and walked back up the narrow *callejon* towards Quebrada I tried to think whether any other conversation in this book had been like this one. I couldn't think of any. To borrow someone else's phrase, I could've called this chapter Lifelong Learning. It was a schooling term from which there could be no graduation. It did not lead to a credential or a degree, only to the next round of study. It was fundamentally a way of being.

CHAPTER EIGHTEEN
CARRIE CAMERON

O n an early afternoon in July I found a place to park across from the Rosewood Hotel and walked up Aldama toward the Hotel Matilda. The Matilda is another modern hostelry, this one more contemporary in design, and built on the site of the old Hotel Jacaranda seven or eight years ago. I recall being surprised that the city fathers had let the rather tired old place be demolished. With vintage buildings in the *el centro area*, usually they're concerned that at least the façade be preserved, but this time the Matilda was able to put up a crisp fresh front at the street, which fit its contemporary interior.

This part of town is close to the nearer end of the Parque Juarez. About half a block up Aldama is a gallery called Galería Buena Vida. Although a series of lively and highly textured landscape paintings done by the owner, Carrie Cameron, line the walls, the primary part of the artistic effort is in her cowboy boots. The line is titled Cock of the Walk Designs and she was waiting for me inside.

We had arranged ourselves comfortably around her desk to start a conversation when three women from Florida came in, one with a husband in tow. Naturally Carrie took time to wait on them and sold two pair of boots.

After that we got started. She was wearing a long sleeveless summer dress and a pair of her boots, the original design she told me, with a cowboy hat. You would never guess she was from anywhere but Texas.

"One of the reasons I wanted to talk to you for this book is that you are a single business woman working in San Miguel. You are not retired, and not volunteering at one of the major charitable organization, as far as I know. Has that been an easy path to follow?"

"Well, as a matter of fact I have been very involved in charitable work here in San Miguel."

"Is that right?"

"In 2014 I became cofounder of the Magic Town Music Festival. Our goal was to raise money for a local charity called Casa de los Angeles. They offer free daycare for single moms and they rely totally on donations. The take care of about a hundred kids every day, four years old and younger."

"Do you think they're looking for volunteers?"

"All the time. It's hard to be in San Miguel and not do something for people. There are so many strong needs here."

"That is a thread that moves all through this book. Just to finish up that question, in becoming a single businesswoman in San Miguel, has that part of your life here been an easy path to follow?"

"Yes. I moved here almost eight years ago. I had first come to this town exactly two years to the day that I moved here. Having an art gallery here, I had been doing that for years in Texas, so that was the easy part. Making custom boots was something I had never even thought about. But all in all it's been a fairly easy process."

"Was that a decision you made after you came here?"

"I thought about it before I moved here on October 30, 2010. I went back to Texas to see my family for Christmas, and I had a driver take me to the airport. He spoke English and I mentioned to him that I was thinking about getting a pair of boots made for myself. He said that his dad was a tanner in León and that he knew everybody. I suggested that when he picked me up on the way back through we could go into León to see if he could set something up for me."

"And León is where the airport is, or quite close to it."

"Exactly. When I returned, it was obvious that the driver hadn't set up a meeting and I never did meet his dad, the "tanner." But we went into León anyway. I had printed up a photo of a painting I had done. We started walking around on the street where everything is all about the leather business, and everybody was telling me, no they couldn't do it. But three people gave me the same man's card, so we called him up. We met with him that afternoon and we've been working together ever since. He's an amazing artisan and he works out of his house."

Carrie Cameron's manner is expressive and often dynamic. She would be hard to misunderstand.

"Do you have employees as such?"

"Yes, I have one assistant here. She's the only employee, but I have many people that I support. For example, all of these cuffs are made in Alcocer." This is a neighborhood behind the Luciérnaga Mall. The table behind me was filled with leather cuffs in a broad range of colors, each with different decorative elements. "It's a group of nine women with little children that sit around a table and make my cuffs. We try to support the Mexican community as much as possible."

"Do you feel that in these eight years San Miguel has become home for you in a fundamental way?"

"In every way." Her broad gesture swept away any other possibility. "I have no desire to leave here or move back to the States. I'll go back to see my family now and then, but I feel so much more comfortable here. I walk everywhere I go. There is such a sense of community in San Miguel. We're also heavily into the music scene here. We support a lot of the musicians; we buy them guitars and drums sets. For example, Paco Rivera is a local musician. Pila Seca is his band. They started out in junior high together. Paco's best friend was just killed in a car wreck. He was thirty years old with a nine-year-old son. The boy has no father now. We're giving money to pay for his schooling. He's in a private school in Querétaro."

Querétaro is a growing city of about 800,000 less than an hour away to the east.

"Please tell me about your boots. Looking around, I see an enormous variety of designs. How are they made and designed? Do you use local resources like artists or leather suppliers?"

"All the leather comes from México. My boot maker lives in León not too far from the leather market, because that's where he gets everything. I would love to have him here in San Miguel, that would be easier for me, but he has to be near his leather sources. I do the design ideas, although I'll work with people too. For example I've got a guy right now who loves the Grateful Dead. He wants all this Grateful Dead stuff on his boots. A skull here, the little dancing bears on the sides. He told me what he wanted. We sat down and drew it all out. We went online and looked up some things. Next thing you know we've got a design for a boot. It's fun, it's easy, and I enjoy it."

"Given that so much of what you sell is custom, how would you describe your inventory? Is it mainly a way of showing customers the range of possible designs?"

"That and money."

"Money?"

"Exactly. I don't owe any money on this inventory and I don't want to get a loan. I prefer to pay as I go. The boots cost me a good chunk of money for each pair. My boot maker works out of his house and does one pair at a time."

"And it's just one man making all these?"

"It's one man doing the drawing, the tooling, and the painting. Then he has two other guys that help him put them together."

"Then would it be correct to say that nearly all of your sales are custom orders?"

"I would say about half."

"So half the customers just come in and buy something right off the shelf."

She smiled at this. "Yes, because so many people want instant gratification, and I've lost many sales because I didn't have what they wanted in the right size. If I could, I would do that, have a bigger inventory."

"In the time you've been doing this, about eight years, do you find there are design trends in this business?"

"Yes, I think that right now I have a lot of people coming in asking me for shorter boots. But still, a cowboy boot is a cowboy boot is a cowboy boot. The people that wear them love them, and I'm one of those people. That's why I started this business in the first place. They are the most comfortable things I can wear. I walk around this town in them all the time."

"Are you a trendsetter yourself in boot design, or are you mainly listening to your customers and responding?"

"I would say that I'm the one with the vision more than the clients. Usually I don't go by too many rules, either. That's one of the reasons I moved to México. There are too many rules in the United States."

"Can you describe your inventory? What is it I'm looking at here?"

"All these boots are custom made by hand. When someone comes in we can measure and fit them exactly. Everything here in my gallery is made in México, except for my hats, and I'm working on a Mexican source for those. My paintings on the wall here are all about México, and that's really my passion. I'd rather sell paintings all day long more than a pair of boots."

"As a businesswoman here have you encountered any problems that you might not have seen in the U.S.?"

"I would say that I don't know if it's any more difficult to get permission to do things here, but for example, I still don't have a sign on my building. I have tried, but my landlord hadn't paid his property taxes, so I had to do that for him before they would give me permission. Then the new mayor came in and they change everything whenever that happens. So, I still don't have a sign and now we're in the process of having another new mayor come in. But then, in the States, it seems like you've got to have a permit to do anything.

"When I first started this business I had a Mexican partner. Without her it would've been much more difficult because she got a lot of things set up and running. She ended up bowing out later on."

"Who is your target customer? Is it a tourist or a local resident?"

"I sell to both, but it's way more to tourists than locals."

"What would you say is the ratio between Mexican and expat customers?"

"It would be much more to gringos."

"What has been the biggest obstacle you've faced here in business?"

This question resulted in a long pause. "Early on, before I really learned the ropes and I was having some issues, I hired a Mexican to work for me, and he ended up attacking me."

"What!"

"It was a really bad situation, a physical attack

and I thought I was going to die. I had lived here only a little over a year when that happened. He stole my passport and my visa, so I couldn't leave. And I would've left after that. It was because of that I became a stronger person. But that was really the only bad thing that's happened to me."

"What's it like dealing with Mexican bureaucracy, like the tax people, for example?"

"In that area I have been very fortunate because my ex business partner had a CPA she'd been working with for years. I still use him, and I never have to call him or anything. He gets it all done for me. That's been very easy. I have worried about being closed down. You see so many businesses getting shut down because of little things. If you're very vocal about the local government, well, it's better to keep your mouth shut."

"When I write these chapters I'm always thinking about who would be interested in reading them. One of the readers looking most closely at this one might be a woman from Canada or the States who's thinking about starting or moving an existing business down here. Imagine that she's trying to put herself in your boots. What would you say to her so that she can be better prepared when she arrives?"

"I feel that it's a pretty close-knit community here, even though there are so many people I still don't know. You have to have an open mind."

"In terms of the way things are done here?"

"Yes. You know, I've been very fortunate in being well respected since I've been here. Everybody knows who I am. Part of that is being a good person that doesn't talk about people behind their backs. If you live here as a single woman, you're always going to be seen as part of this or that group, and I really try to stay away from that. To me, that was something that I moved away from when I left Texas. If you're here to start a business you have to know what you're doing, so you need to do some research."

"To some degree it might be a man having those same considerations as well. Do you think the problems men would face might be different because of their gender? Or is that not so much an issue?"

"No, I think that's totally true. Rusty, my partner, moved here before I did and we met here. He had control of the local airport. He's a professional airport engineer and flight instructor. When he moved here it was only a dirt runway. Over the years he was able to get it paved. Then the local government came in and kicked him off the project. Since then he's been trying to get it reopened, but it's all about bureaucracy. Now he's got about $50,000 of his own money into the project, plus years and years of work. He has really run into some difficult things. So yes, I think if you're a strong-willed man trying to do business here it can be difficult."

"So being a sturdy male is not necessarily a plus."

"No, I think it's difficult to do business here as a man. Of course, what he's doing has to do with the government, and they don't ever want gringos telling them what to do."

"How would your business be different if you were operating it in Texas?"

"There would be a lot more paperwork. I actually had my business based in Texas when I moved here, since I still had the gallery there. So I just made this business a division of Carrie Cameron Art. Then we shut down the gallery in Dallas."

"And that was an art gallery up there, all paintings."

"Yes, and it was so much work every month keeping things separated between México and Texas. I called my CPA in Texas one day and asked her, 'What is the advantage of keeping this business going in Texas?' and she said, 'Really, there's nothing. You don't have to do this.'

"So I shut that business down. Now that has just simplified my life like you wouldn't believe. It's wonderful. I don't owe anybody any money, and I pay all my bills in cash. It has made things a whole lot easier."

"So I think I know the answer to this final question. Would you do this again?"

"Of course!"

We shook hands as I said goodbye. As I left I stepped aside for a couple of women who were looking through the door. The boots had a rich leathery smell that beckoned to people passing. Walking back to my car I thought about Carrie Cameron's clear-sighted view of what she wanted and how to get there. It was a niche business she had carved out herself, one ideally fitted to San Miguel and México.

Of course, part of her success had to be that the concept and design of those boots were exclusive and original. That would be a plus wherever she had set up the gallery. The customers passing by would know they had never seen boots just like this. If they were in the mood to buy a unique memento of their San Miguel trip, the Galería Buena Vida was a perfect place to find it.

CHAPTER NINETEEN
ALAN GOLDFARB

On the busy thoroughfare of the Ancha de San Antonio as it becomes the Celaya road there's an intersection that's grown into a hot spot in the last few years. A popular delicatessen has relocated there across from the branch of a fashionable bakery. Behind them is a newish hotel and convention center. Across the Ancha several restaurants are flourishing. I have walked or driven past this part of town a thousand times, I'm sure, without noticing the anonymous cul-de-sac that opens onto the street. Nothing about it draws the eye. It's no more than a vacancy in a hopping urban scene.

It was the late morning of a bright day in early August after the ruthless rains of June had yielded to an unusually dry July. About fifty meters inside the cul-de-sac the studio of Alan Goldfarb occupies a white building without any signage. As I approached, a dog stationed in the doorway tried to convince me I had come to the wrong place, but I'm not easily deterred when I'm in search of a good conversation. I had known Alan for some years but not very well. I thought what we mostly had in common was our experience in woodworking.

I had operated a cabinet shop in Saint Paul for about twenty years, although cabinets as such were not my business. In those twenty years I had built no more than about eight kitchens, and those only if I needed the work. More often my crew and I built custom furniture to my designs, constructed paneled libraries in upscale homes (often with secret doors and coffered ceilings), and crafted classic restaurant interiors, like the mahogany landmark in Minneapolis, The Times Bar (1982). Eventually I had burned out on it, but it was still a creative and challenging time that I look back on fondly, even as I know now that I'd rather be writing.

Alan Goldfarb relocated the dog to a less stressful place in a different room and let me in. The surroundings looked more than familiar. The table saw, jointer, wide belt sander, surface planer, and drill press were all linked by a custom-built dust collection system. It was a place made for serious woodworking, right down to the hardwood planks leaning ready against the wall. He gave me a brief tour before we sat down to talk.

"How did you get involved with woodworking?" I began. "Was that your original field?"

"No, it all started when I was thirteen years old growing up in the suburbs of New York City, in Westchester County. Most of the adults in that town pursued one of three occupations. There were the businessmen who road the commuter trains to office work in the city, and the townees, who did the local blue-collar jobs like being a plumber or running the butcher shop. The third option was employment at the new world headquarters of IBM, the first big corporate campus in the area, located on a large hill overlooking town.

"I was fortunate to attend a high school where I was exposed to a lot of art through frequent field trips to the museums in the city. At that young age I was reading Gandhi and Khalil Gibran, and I had a kind of spiritual experience during which I realized I would not pursue any of those three conventional careers, but that I would pursue some kind of creative work, working with my hands as an artist or craftsman.

"I first I learned to make wheel thrown ceramic pottery. That took me to kiln firing, and from there I was exposed to glassblowing. When I was sixteen I got an after school job apprenticing to a glassblower, and when I was eighteen I finished high school and apprenticed to another glassblower up in the Berkshires."

Alan is a man of average height with a white ponytail. He had told me during the shop tour that he was fifty-nine. His manner is at once dynamic and thoughtful. I was sure he had considered many of my questions long before, since I sent them to him in advance.

"This is starting to sound like the woodworking

was one step on a longer path of development," I said, "the way one thing evolves into another and then another."

"In the late 1970s, after a period of apprenticeship, I studied glassblowing at the School for American Craftsmen at RIT in Rochester, New York. From there I was apprenticed to glass artists in the San Francisco Bay Area. Later I studied with Dale Chihuly and a number of other international glass artists masters at the Pilchuck Glass School in Washington. In 1983 I moved to Burlington, Vermont where I built a studio and had a twenty-five year career as a glassblower.

"I had a small team of apprentices and we would blow about a thousand pieces of glass a year, then finish them by grinding and polishing. We'd load all of that and a portable display into a van and travel to six different cities to do high-end craft fairs every year. Pieces of my work made it into some notable galleries and private collections and several museums. My greatest validation as an object maker came in 2000 when The Smithsonian Institution purchased a group of my pieces. I kept up that routine for twenty-three years until I reached a state of mental, physical, and financial exhaustion, and just couldn't keep going."

"You were looking for a way out."

"At that time quite accidentally I visited San Miguel, and like many of the expats here, I fell in love with the place and moved here. It offered another unconventional lifestyle, just as being a studio craftsman had. I did this deep internal quest that led to a very simple conclusion: I just needed to continue to make stuff. I started doing carpentry, building chicken coops, and very slowly came back into studio work. I was looking for a ceramic venue and I went to several of the group studios here in San Miguel, but there really wasn't an opening for me. But when I came to this woodworking studio, there was an opening for me. So it was kind of arbitrary that I ended up working in wood."

I thought about this for a moment. "Are you suggesting that you got into woodworking mainly because the equipment was here?" That would've been a rare degree of serendipity.

He smiled at this idea. "I was of that generation of glass workers that made all of their own equipment. Now you would have a furnace builder come in and build it for you, but that wasn't available to me then. I built my own furnaces and ovens for melting glass. Other skills I learned in the course of building the shop fixtures included steelwork and welding, along with carpentry and woodworking. So that was where I first developed an interest in wood."

"So you are essentially self-taught?"

"Basically, until I came here. Then I worked for a seventy-two-year old Mexican master carpenter who taught me to make doors for six months, and a retired guitar maker from Santa Monica came in and taught me to make boxes for another six months."

"More apprenticeships. When we spoke earlier about doing this conversation, you told me you had more recently gotten into painting. What led to that?"

"My early carpentry took me to woodworking, which took me more recently to sculpting wood. In the process of being an untrained sculptor I injured my wrist. It's a severe arthritis of the small bones, so I can't hold the vibrating tools anymore."

"Is this like a Dremel?" Dremel is a small hand-held grinding tool that accommodates a wide assortment of bits.

"Heavy tools, more like body grinders and power sanders."

"So it's much larger in scale."

"Right. But because I was able to see my creative arc still remained intact, even after five years of working with wood and then having an injury, I realized that even if I switched materials, that creative arc would still be in motion."

"And you could get similar rewards."

"Yes, but more specifically, when I started pigmenting the carved wood pieces, I realized that my ability to use paint was ten years behind my skill at sculpting objects. I thought, 'I need to get back into working with colors and do some painting.'"

"One of the most rewarding things I always felt about working with my hands in both painting and wood-working, which of course intimately involves the creative mind as well, was that there was a physical object in front of me when it was finished, an artifact. Do you look at it that way?"

"Not really. I mean, I am attached to the object while making it, but the vast majority of the finished objects just seem like dusty relics to me. There are only a few that are special enough to retain their magic. For me, the way it goes is that if I'm making a piece of some kind and it doesn't go well, it brings me down and I get upset. I get tired and it takes more energy to go on. If it's going well it gives me a lift and pushes me onward.

"The fact is that I am so wedded to the process of making objects that most of them do not contain that much interest for me once they're finished. My real reward is learning and growing in the creative process. Making a superb object is a kind of frustrating ambition. My real reward is learning and growing while being in the flow of the creative process.

"Here's an example from my glassmaking days. I would blow glass about five days a week, forty-five weeks a year. That's like two hundred and twenty-five days a year. At random, for about a hundred of those days, I'd be trying as hard as I could to have the pieces come together and work. It would be frustrating and exhausting, something like having a bad toothache while slogging through a muddy swamp in heavy fog.

"For about another hundred days things would have a better rhythm and the pieces would come together with competence. Then about twenty of those days would be elevated, as if my team and I were working together with some degree of mastery. That would be fulfilling and spur us on. But for those remaining five days we would achieve a cruising altitude where it was like we were channeling pure spirit. The work would be absolutely transcendental and we would make pieces of such an elevated aesthetic that we could hardly believe they had come from our hands. So out of a thousand pieces a year there would be maybe a dozen that would be absolutely incredible. Like you're saying, I would be attached to those. The rest were ordinary."

"Would you still sell those dozen, just like you sold all the others?" Of the approximately two hundred and seventy-five paintings I had done, there were about half a dozen that I would buy back any time without hesitation.

"My intention was to archive those because they were so special, and I would keep them for as long as I could. But makers and collectors alike could see they were exquisite and I could get five times the normal price for them. I was always a better craftsman than businessman, so inevitably many of them were sold when I came under financial pressure."

"How many of those iconic pieces to you still have today?"

"To be honest with you, an odd detail of my career is that after producing about 20,000 pieces of glass, I no longer own a single one of them. Not even a shard. But fortunately a very close friend and collector purchased my archive entirely at the end of my career, so they're in good hands. That gave me the money to move to San Miguel."

Around us, where there was no equipment or lumber against the walls, large scale drawings were hung like ideas for work in progress.

"I am looking now at your most recent painting. It's a frog on a background that is...how would you describe it?"

"It's a pattern of dots in space. It's not black and white like op art, but it's got a little op art thing going on. If I had to classify it I would say it's in the genre of old rock and roll posters, psychedelic or visionary artwork."

"Summer of love?"

"Yes, there's a little Haight Ashbury going on there. It also references the indigenous shamanic tradition."

"And here in the state of Guanajuato, the frog is an important symbol. So the technique is one of layering the colors from dark to light, outside in, and that dictates your process."

"Yes, and you can see that process if you look back on old wallpaper from the 1960s. There were bands of color. A lot of times it appeared in shades of orange and 'harvest gold,' and brown."

"Are you at a point of thinking about marketing these pictures?"

"This painting is very new, and I'm using brushes for the first time now, but I have sold some of the previous poured paintings."

"Do you set goals for yourself as you work, or is it more of a natural evolution where one thing determines the next and you don't see what's coming that far ahead?"

"Both of those. I combine that as one process. Some of the things I learn from going towards a goal dictate the next, unforeseen, step. But I am very goal oriented and committed to a regular work ethic. I work a lot of hours a year."

"You said earlier you had been down here for eleven years now. Is it home?"

Alan hesitated for a long moment. "You know, that's a complex question for me."

"I think it is for most people. It's a thread that runs through this book."

"A lot of people move on, like in the way they call

geographic cures, when their life gets screwed up. I've never moved in that way. When I went to Burlington, Vermont when I was out of school, I was there for twenty-three years. I came to San Miguel for eleven years, as I said. But as you know, San Miguel is changing dramatically. We have now both tremendous gentrification and a huge population increase. It is no longer an inexpensive place to live, although I've been lucky and found here both a living and a studio situation that are very economical. But overall, it's become one of the most expensive places in México. In the beginning of my time here I was so taken with the amazing high desert sunlight, the magic of Mexican culture. The people not being dependent on materialism for their sense of well being."

"Or in another word, consumerism," I said.

"Yes, it was enchanting and healing to be in a culture that valued all those sacred rituals, the parades and the festivals like the Day of the Dead. At first it was great to be around people that move more slowly, but now, like when I go to a service counter, perhaps at the electric company, for example, I can see that it's going to eat my morning."

"You mentioned a while ago about the population increase the town is going through. Is it a different kind of expat who is moving down here now than it was eleven years ago when you came?"

"Historically different kinds of expats have come here, like the wave after World War II where they were coming down on the GI Bill to study art. In the 1970s it was more the hippies, and Neil Cassidy died here."

"Yes, they found him out on the railroad tracks in 1968. He was more the Beat Generation."

"Then in the 1980s girls from Boston would come down here to get some bullfighting posters and try to meet a matador. After that it became a retirement community. Historically the demographic of the people coming here has changed. In terms of my opinion about how I feel toward people now, you know, there's a thing that happens. I was never a big Grateful Dead head, but I was a little Grateful Dead head, and I followed them. There was a time when the old timers would be saying, 'Damn, where's the sense of reverence, I hate the new people coming in!' So I think that is something people do regardless of the milieu. There's a frustration with newcomers."

"Is it like, please lock the door after me?"

"These are really good questions, not only for here, but other places in the world. I think that's what a lot of people would like, and that's what's happening with Trump. He'd like to lock the door and not let any immigrants in. Maybe we'd like to lock the door and not let the new type of San Miguel residents in. One of the quotes I heard about San Miguel when I got here was this, 'San Miguel: the place where nobody's a stranger but everybody's a little strange.'"

"I have another one. You're here either because you're wanted or because you're not wanted."

He nodded at this. "I don't know if strange is that good a word, but not everybody is cut out to be an expat. It takes a certain kind of person to forego the comfort and convenience, and the consumerism of the United States. To live confronted with a different value system, where things are much slower. But I am frustrated by the number of wealthy Mexicans and some of the new gringos here. Yet, that's the kind of gentrification that's happening all over the world. I have a cousin living in Cambodia. She's been living there a long time. She said that her town has become gentrified. You can get gluten-free meals in restaurants there now, wheat grass or whatever. She can't believe it."

"To wrap this up, what's waiting out there next for you in that creative arc, a phrase I like very much. Or is there too much potential for painting to even think of that?"

"What I'm in the midst of doing now is immersing myself in a several year period of creative development where I produce a body of related work that includes drawings, paintings, and wood carvings, then I will look for a gallery where I can do a show."

"I think you said you're fifty-nine now?"

"Right."

"Does this process go on forever, until you simply pitch forward into a wet canvas? I don't see retirement in your arc."

"Well, when I moved into this studio, I said to a colleague I had in here at that time, 'They're going to carry me out of here in an urn.' But the fact is that over the last five years the gentrification around here has been ferocious with all these new businesses. I'm concerned that I'll be squeezed out of this neighborhood.

"But you wouldn't quit."

"No. I would be forced to seek out a less expensive place to be."

We shook hands and said goodbye.

As I left and reached the humming traffic out on the thoroughfare, I realized how welcome it was to have another in depth conversation with someone about the creative process. Kay Lynne Sattler had made me feel the same way. It's normally very personal and individual, and too often creative people are unable to express themselves clearly about what it is they really do. Sometimes they simply find no reason to be introspective about it. When it works, if it works, that's all that many need. I was grateful that Alan was such an astute observer of the trail he'd made through life.

What interested me so much was that the creative path he had traveled was quite different from mine even as, in the cases of painting and woodworking, it ranged over much of the same terrain. I felt like there ought to be some squib from Asian philosophy that would express this, but I couldn't think what it might be.

CHAPTER TWENTY
NORY CONTRACTOR & PATRONATO PRO NIÑOS

The quarter of town called Ignacio Ramirez lies slightly offset and behind the Tuesday Market. It's not a high traffic area and on a Wednesday morning in early August I was able to find a parking place with no problem just outside the gate of the Patronato pro Niños headquarters. It was not a neighborhood I was familiar with, although it's not far from the Querétaro Road.

This was no improvised facility for a newly established charity. It's a four square two story modern building in the contemporary style. It was clearly purpose built as a combined medical dental clinic and administrative headquarters for an organization dedicated to providing base line health care for all the young children in the *municipio* who might lack it. Of course, while this facility illustrates the seriousness of the Patronato effort, it does not begin to address the substantial ongoing costs of healthcare delivery itself. For that, Patronato still depends every day on the financial contributions of the San Miguel community.

Inside in the lobby a dozen or so kids waited quietly with one of their parents for their appointments. As I stood surveying the scene Nory Contractor emerged from one of the offices and introduced herself. She is an energetic woman in her mid fifties who runs this major healthcare provider for the children of this part of México. With a paid staff of around two dozen, they do not charge a single centavo for their services.

We found a quieter zone in the conference room upstairs and settled at the end of a long table.

"In some of the notes you sent me about your background you mentioned you were born in Cuba and came to Miami at the age of six. As we sit here today in San Miguel, doesn't that mean you've gone through the experience of expat adjustment twice?"

"Yes, and it was almost surreal being here as an immigrant at the immigration office applying for my residency visa. It was a very different experience for me, but I don't recall the first one, I was too young."

"Have you been back to Cuba since you left as a child?"

"No, but as a matter of fact, next year, March of 2019, will mark my fiftieth anniversary of having left. My husband and I are planning a trip back there during January and February, and the real reason for that is to scout some destinations. I have many Patronato Pro

Niños supporters who would like to go on a trip with a Cuban to support our organization. We're going to be working with a sister organization in Cuba."

"So you're almost like a tour guide."

"We also do a number of tours here. Now we're working on having a tour group of dentists from Canada."

"And you have family still in Cuba?"

"Many of them. My father is one of eleven children, and he has eight brothers and sisters still in Cuba."

"You have a lot of cousins."

"Too many."

Nory Contractor has a lively and often emphatic manner. I began to suspect that her management of this organization came easily to her, and she must've had earlier administrative experience.

"San Miguel is known for its expat community of Canadians and Americans. Is Miami like that for Cubans?"

"In my opinion it was like that in the sixties when we arrived. Now Miami is the greatest melting pot in the world. Just yesterday I mentioned to someone that I had worked as the president of a small college in Miami. I had ninety faculty members there and they represented more than thirty countries."

"Amazing! What would a life in healthcare or healthcare education have been like had you stayed in

Cuba?"

"Well, there is an interesting TED talk about Cuban medical schools. Right now they are ranked in the top five in the world. Medical education there is really advanced. The problem with healthcare in Cuba is that it's not available to the common people. It is available to people who come in with dollars. So if you're a Cuban living there and you have something as simple as diabetes, the chances are you're going to have to buy your medications in the black market."

"Really."

"And there's a TED talk on that as well."

"That's amazing. So with healthcare education being that good, is it mostly drawing students from outside of Cuba?"

"Absolutely."

"And then they don't stay to practice?"

"Right, they don't stay, and as a matter of fact, I was consulting for many years with a medical university in the Dominican Republic. It was a family owned business that had been around for more than fifty years. All of their children went to school in different parts of the world, and one of them went to the University of Cuba in my own hometown of Camaguey.

"Then later you ended up in San Miguel. What brought you into this position as the head of Patronato?"

"When I first came to San Miguel in March of

2015 I was still working as a higher education consultant in Miami. Shortly after getting here one of my clients decided that he needed me there for two weeks out of every month. I was basically staying there for two weeks and then staying in San Miguel for two weeks. I did that for nine months. It got old very fast. I was fortunate that my husband told me about this opening at Patronato. I applied, since my background fit the position really well in a lot of different ways. I went through a number of stages in an interesting interview process. Many of the people were from the board of directors. Last week marked two years for me here."

"When you were consulting in healthcare higher education, who typically would come to you as a client?"

"There were a lot of different clients. I've been doing that since 1998. Most recently there was a group that came to us that owns twenty-three campuses of universities in Peru. They decided they wanted to open a university in Miami. In May we inaugurated that campus. For two years before that we worked on getting all the documentation they needed for the Department of Education to approve it."

"That was their certification."

"Right. There is a Commission of Independent Education. It's the one that approves private proprietary schools."

"So this all had to be set up in accordance with

their rules."

"The rule book is quite large and I know it very well. Because of all the compliance and regulatory background that I have, it's very easy for me to apply a lot of that here, and although we're in another country, there's still a department of health here. There are still many labor laws that govern employees here. It's been a good match."

"I can see where for you, with your Spanish speaking background, your higher education background, your medical background, there probably aren't many people around who could offer the set of qualifications that you have."

"We're very fortunate here in San Miguel to have a bank of intelligent young professionals, much younger than I am, but I did bring to the table some skills you might normally have needed several other people to provide, especially the bilingual part."

"Most of your life has been spent in the States. Could we say then that what prompted you to come to México was the opportunity your husband had identified here at Patronato?"

"At first we had no idea about Patronato, although we wanted to live somewhere else than the U.S."

"Is he Cuban?"

"No, he's Jewish American from New York. He lived in Miami since he was a teenager. We both love

Miami, but it is a busy and expensive city. My husband was in the art business. He had a gallery there. Then he decided that he just wanted to deal in art and he continued to do that, buying and selling and participating in auctions."

"Do you have children there?"

"Yes, I have one child, a young woman who's married and a professional, and my husband has one of his three sons living there."

"Would it be correct to say that San Miguel has become home for you now?"

"San Miguel is home for me. It's definitely where my heart is. I thank God every day that I'm part of this incredible institution. It was hard at the beginning to feel anchored here. I loved the city but I still kept feeling that Miami was home. When I became involved with Patronato that changed a lot. I felt that if I wasn't here and doing what I'm here for, then something was missing."

"It appears that your roots in healthcare education go back a long way. What attracted you to that field?"

"I first got into healthcare education as a professor. I decided I was going to teach anatomy and physiology, and I did for a number of years at a college. Then I became the chair of the program at that college. I continued to grow in the administrative ranks until I became president of that college. On a personal level that's something I'm very proud of, since I come from a family where my Cuban parents didn't have an opportunity for education. My father was one of eleven children, and he only went through fifth grade. My mother, one of six, went through sixth grade. So for me, not only graduating from a university but being president of a college was a big accomplishment."

"You must've been focused on that from an early age."

"When I was growing up, John, my parents never stressed education. My siblings did not finish high school. This is where I came to believe that we're all born with a little chip that points us in some direction. For me, that was education. That is still a big value for me. I am also involved in Jóvenes Adelante. Do you know about them?"

"They send worthy kids to college. I have a chapter in this book about them and Sue Leonard."

"Wonderful. I'm a mentor there."

"Perfect!"

"I think education is the way out of a lot of situations that we deal with here. It's the best way to get people out of the poverty level where they're living."

"What is your day like at Patronato, here in this lovely and quite recent building?"

"Our facility is ten years old. We're very fortunate to have it. It came from the effort of a board of directors that has always been very strong. We had the land donated and we raised the funds for the building. My hat is always off to the board. But I don't think I have two single days in any month that are the same. The clinic here is open every day from eight A.M. until one P.M. Our four mobile units leave here every day at seven A.M. I get up at six-thirty every morning and put my phone on. Many times I start getting calls at six forty-five. When the crew arrives here a number of things can happen. I'll often be on the phone with them. We do have leaders in each area. So my days are never the same."

"Your drivers on these medical vans, are they making a regular circuit that takes them through a set scheduled set of villages in the course of a week or a month?"

"Let me tell you how that works. We have a very set way of handling which communities we will be at. It's something that we plan at the beginning of the year. I have a director of the dental program and of the medical program. Even my lead driver sits in on these discussions, because based on our previous experience we map out where we're going to be at any given time. When we go to a community we stay there, returning to base every day, until all the children are seen. If we go into a community where there are two hundred kids and we can do ten of them a day, we know we'll be there twenty days."

"And so you would routinely see every child in

that community?" I hadn't realized that their focus had such depth.

"Yes. The problem we're facing right now is that we only have four vans. Two are dental only, they're the older ones, and the two new ones are both medical and dental. One of those is dedicated to the thirty-five communities where Feed the Hungry has kitchens."

"They're in this book too."

"Those kids have about twenty-eight percent better oral health than the others, on average, because of their diet. The other three vans are handling the other remaining five hundred communities. So our average return time to those communities is three and a half years."

"What would the organization like to do that it is not able to do now?"

"Our goal and campaign is what we call, Every Child, Every Year. We'd like to get to the point where we can provide at least one medical and one dental checkup each year for every child in the *municipio* of San Miguel."

"To do that would involve drastically increasing the frequency..."

"By increasing the number of vans, and the number of doctors and dentists."

"Among the children you treat what do you find to be the most common problems?"

She shook her head slowly. "There are two sets of children that we treat. There are the routine children, and they're coming for a normal medical or dental checkup. Then we have the other set of children, the extreme cases. The first group is almost seven thousand children. The extreme cases this year were almost at two hundred fifty children. I know those numbers sound hugely different, but I can tell you that the cost for the seven thousand is minimal compared to the cost for the two hundred fifty. Those children are often suffering from epilepsy, cerebral palsy, Down syndrome, and autism. They require a lot of rehabilitative treatment. Many require both motor skills and language therapy. We also provide transportation to hospitals in León, Mexico City, and Uruapan."

"I was about to ask you about hospitalization. Who pays for that?"

"We do, in conjunction with Seguro Popular." This is a government sponsored hospitalization program for low-income people. "For all of our children who receive that benefit, they cannot be on private insurance. Many of them who have that coverage need to be hospitalized. The problem is that hospitals in every city are provided by the government based on the population. So places with smaller populations will have a hospital whose reach of specialties is not very broad. If I have a child who is a burn victim, they will have to go to Mexico City. We provide the transportation, and sometimes we even provide the hotel space for the family."

"And how large is your staff?"

"Twenty-three.'

"Does Patronato look for volunteers, and if so, what kind of skills are you in need of?"

"We have a lot of volunteers now focused on the talented group who are our Historical Walking Tour guides. We run that program out of *el centro* three times a week, Monday, Wednesday, and Friday. Then we have an architectural tour too. That program accounts for about twenty-five percent of our income. Now we're in the process of doing a call out to the community for other types of volunteerism. We need some help here in the office, and we always need more help when we have events. That would be everything from pre-event ticket sales, to acquiring donations, sponsorships, and setting up events."

"You told me that twenty-five percent of your funding comes from your walking tours. Where does the rest come from?"

"The largest percentage comes from private donors, both Canadian and American, and some other foreigners. We're also developing a donor base of Mexicans, which has not been historically large for us. More recently we've also been working on local businesses as part of our donor program. We also apply for government grants."

"Do you have competition in your walking tours from individuals operating for profit?"

"We have some competition in so far as some folks don't understand the basis of where their donation is going. There are some private people doing walking tours, and I always say there's a slice of the pie for everybody. Usually whenever a potential walking tour guest realizes where our proceeds go, then they're happy to choose us."

"What's the most rewarding part of your role in all of this?"

"When I see a child where I really believe we have saved their life. Here's an example. Last year in April we had a volunteer who brought in a little girl. She was four years old and she was being carried by her parents, as she had been for about a year and a half. They didn't know what was wrong with her, only that she used to walk but no longer could. Our doctor here raised the possibility that she had leukemia. We sent her to a regional hospital in León, where she was confirmed as a leukemia patient. She has now gone through extensive chemo, and she's not only walking but running."

"She's in remission."

"Yes, and she's my little angel. We adore her and she calls me grandma. That is my greatest thrill, when we can save a child's life."

"I was surprised to see that Patronato is forty-eight years old this year. How did it get its start? It seems like back then there were few expats here. A lot of times we tend to think that these organizations were founded by expats, but that's not always the case, is it? Was it founded by local Mexicans?"

"We are now getting prepared for our fiftieth anniversary celebration. It's going to take a great deal of preparation. We did some research too, and last week I met a woman named Maria Williams. She was one of the founders of this organization forty-eight years ago. She's still here in San Miguel, and she was married to George Williams."

"I'm sure I have met her, too."

"She's an amazing woman. You would not believe the stories that she has. And she is Mexican, although she spent many years in the U.S. She and Ted Gravenson, James Mullen, Noma Cayton, and Daniel Mojica Vazquez started Patronato as a program to help children they saw in the streets to go to school. It was not founded as a healthcare organization. They wanted to get the kids school books, shoes, a couple of pencils, and notepads. As the government funding for schools got better they realized that the real area of need, especially in the remote regions, was healthcare. In those days a lot of children suffered from cleft palate and lip. A huge effort was made in educating the mothers as to what they could do to prevent this problem. In those days there were forty or fifty cases a year locally. Now we have about four, five or six cases."

"So it's been cut by nearly ninety percent. If you

weren't working with Patronato here, what else might you be doing?"

"For sure I would be involved in other wonderful organizations here, such as Feed the Hungry or Jóvenes Adelante. I'm also involved with the Midday Rotary Club. I would always choose to be involved with some kind of community service."

I said goodbye to Nory Contractor and found my car. I had much the same sensation that I'd had coming away from Feed the Hungry. Patronato Pro Niños was a carefully focused, businesslike program with a great deal of momentum. They were unblinkingly pursuing an enormous task as they filled a critical need in this community.

CHAPTER TWENTY-ONE
COLLEEN SORENSON

The Guadalupe neighborhood lies along the edge of the Calzada la Aurora on the northwestern end of San Miguel. Across the Calzada is the Fabrica la Aurora, a great resource of art venues and antique shops that we encountered earlier during the chapter focused on the ceramic artist Kay Lynne Sattler.

In the earlier years of my tenure in San Miguel, colonia Guadalupe was a solid working class neighborhood with limited numbers of expats, but over time, it's become known as an arts district with studio tours and festivals. If the invasion of artists of different kinds has not precisely gentrified it, since they typically find themselves more at home in Bohemia than in Mayfair, it has still altered the tone and feel of the area. Nothing displays this change more vividly than the large-scale murals that cover many walls distributed along the streets. It's a place where a walking tour is a rewarding way to spend a few hours.

I arrived in Guadalupe on a Sunday morning in August with an appointment to see Colleen Sorenson and have a conversation about her life in San Miguel, and her role in changing the face of the neighborhood where she lived. When I was met at her door by her dog, Elton (middle name, John), Colleen appeared to show me inside. It's a U-shaped building enclosing a paved court-yard, a space that looked like it might have been used for parking at some time in the past. This court is faced by a number of doors, and once Colleen led me inside, where the rooms also flow from one into the other, the distinc-tion was often not clear whether I was in a living space or an art studio. It suggested a kind of happy overlap for a resident to whom the boundary between art and life might not always be clear.

The same could be said for some writers.

Colleen is a tall, active woman in her mid sixties. Both her comments and her manner express the kind of resilience that suggest she's taken her share of hits and is not afraid of taking a few more. I suggested that if we can still learn at all, once we hit a certain age, it is often by our willingness to fall down if required. The lesson lies mainly in the expression on our face as we get up.

We settled into a small sitting room with big cups of freshly brewed coffee.

"Please start with some background about what you did in your past life and how you came to settle in San Miguel."

"I grew up in Minneapolis and attended the

Minneapolis College of Art and Design. After that I was off to New York City, where fashion design was not my kind thing, since I'm not a competitive person. Then I went on to Colorado, and later I lived in Chicago, and that was all cold country. Eventually I ended up in San Antonio, Texas. It was because of my last year in Minneapolis, when there was a wind chill of sixty-some degrees below zero, that I decided that no one should live like that."

This was a conclusion I identified with.

"At the time when my daughter was in about second grade, I went to San Antonio, which was where my family lived, and we lived there until I reached the point when I could not take one more south Texas summer. Here the climate is just perfect."

I considered this for a moment relative to our so deeply flooded month of June. Everything is relative.

"The reason I really left was that I found myself in an unbearably controlling and suffocating environment. I had also been vilified for a project I did with street artists. I felt forced away, so I left San Antonio. And it's affordable here."

"And how long have you been here?"

"It's been eight and a half years now."

"That would put your arrival at some point in 2009. After that long here, do you ever still find yourself being surprised by how things happen in México?"

"Not anymore. My first couple years down here were really tough. I hadn't come here because I wanted to and I had no idea what I was going to do or how I was going to fit in. It's gorgeous here with all kinds of interesting people and so many things going on, but it took time for me to figure it out. On top of all this, my family was very angry with me for moving to México. One could say they were not fans. Muros en Blanco (the neighborhood murals project) settled all that for me. I knew I was meant to stay. It was also at the same time I became involved with social justice issues in the U.S."

"And you started the Muros en Blanco program?"

"I did, because in 2012 was when the tagging started. It happened very fast. There had been *muro* festivals all over the world, and local kids were saying, 'What about us?' But it always starts with the tagging. It was creeping up the Ancha de San Antonio, and it just exploded. So I said to myself, Here I go again! I found out that street art of any kind was not permitted in San Miguel. It's not legal. That's what started it."

"We're going to get into that more in a minute, but first I'd like to talk some about your own art that I see on the walls around us, particularly these tiled panels that appear to be graffiti based."

A broad smile came over her face. "I had started playing with clay and making tiles when my daughter was just a baby. It was therapeutic. I was applying my own tile to furniture and walls. In Texas, I had an arts organization there working with kids at risk. They made their own tile for public art projects. There was a kid there who went by the name of Supher, like suffer. Different spelling. He was in trouble for painting words where he shouldn't have and did his community service with us. He painted a 16' x 4' piece titled Juventud and I applied my tiling. It was purchased by the University of Texas San Antonio. We then did another project that kept him from going to prison. This is what I brought with me. I've been tiling graffiti art ever since."

I studied the series of tiled panels. She had custom made tiles in the shapes and sizes that fit the graffiti letters and graphics.

"This is the project we did together that kept Supher from going to prison. I brought it all down here with me. When people saw it they said to me, 'That's what you need to do here!' That was before Muros en Blanco."

"What is it that has made San Miguel feel like home for you over these eight and a half years, if it does?"

"The street art project did that because I knew I had found the right purpose. A wise and delightful woman named Edith (she recently died at age 100) told me, 'Life is no fun without something going on. You're someone who needs to be involved, you need a purpose.' She was right but it wasn't going to happen in Texas.

When I learned street art of any kind was illegal here, that became my purpose. I had learned the hard way about censorship so this was very personal."

"Let's get into that a little further. I know that the wall painting project is one of your passions. How did that get started? You said earlier that it just fell into your lap."

"When the tagging started happening, people on the Civil List (a community bulletin board) were going wild because it was showing up on homes and businesses, rock walls and churches. At the time I had a tile workshop at the library. Ali Zerriffi had come over to my house and seen the tiled graffiti and he said, 'Colleen, this is what the kids want.' He introduced me to Filip Lein. He's the head of San Miguel Siempre Hermoso (Always Beautiful). That's a public and private group that paints out graffiti. I thought that was fine, but this was a problem that was not going to go away. I told Filip that we need a place for legal street art. There are festivals happening all over Europe, South America, and the United States, so what about San Miguel? There is no painting allowed in *el centro* because of UNESCO World Heritage regulations. I have been to lots of meetings where they were trying to figure out how to get these people, the tourists, out of the *jardín*, and into the neighborhoods. I sat down and made a proposal. I had just moved into this neighborhood, which had also been hit hard by the tagging. It was a working class neighborhood with a great location, across from *el centro*. You can go right over to the Fabrica la Aurora, and you can come back through the Artisans' Market.

"That was four mayors back, but when Mauricio Trejo came in as mayor, things began to move. Maria José Garrido was director of tourism. She had lived in Miami. She was very young and had a lot of energy She had come across my proposal about creating an area for legal painting, and to bring in the best artists from around México. Then these kids would have something to look up to, and they could turn their energy toward art rather than vandalism."

Colleen's attempts to discover reasons for the tagging had gotten nothing coherent in response. I always tended to look at it as an act of power from the powerless, a way of saying, "Hey, I'm here!" Either that or gang symbols in some situations.

"I did get them to understand not to tag on the painted walls, once they were up. It's a respect thing, but there needed to be legal places to paint. For this, permission must be obtained from the property owner and the finished murals must be respected. Maria José and Mayor Mauricio Trejo were interested in tourism. She said to me, 'OK, we will give you the permission, if you'll do a festival.' It took almost a year to get it. I just said 'OK,' without thinking about it. Whatever it took to get the permission. And the reason this has gone forward, because it's been since 2013, so five years now, was that it was done for the right reason. It was necessary. The support was a combination of the municipal authorities, who provided paint, materials and a huge amount of promotion, the Mexican neighbors who offered the walls of their homes and businesses, and the expat neighbors who kept all the artists well fed and housed for three days. That weekend was pure magic."

"How do people get chosen to do one of these murals?"

"Two local artists did all the inviting in 2013. They coordinated all the murals. I took care of covering the food and housing. Everyone came through; it really belongs to the entire neighborhood."

"How many murals are there now?"

"There have been probably 130 painted by now, including the paint-overs."

"Which leads to my next question. How are they maintained?"

"The only mural maintained is the one belonging to Via Orgánica. The artist, Lilliana Zuppini, lives here in colonia San Antonio so she continues to touch up with her acrylics when areas begin to peel. For the rest of the murals, the artists call it 'the life of a wall.' Many murals are still here since 2013 and the artists love that. Some are up only for a few weeks. The main reason they change is because of construction. Another is what the surface is. If a mural is painted on the local chalky paint, the first rain will put moisture behind it and it will begin peeling. Another reason is sometimes people simply want a change. Where the images really live is on the Internet."

I considered this for a moment. My assumption was that something as creative and notable as a mural would be designed to last as long as possible. They could be varnished over with a weatherproof finish that would be renewed as often as required. But as I thought about it, I realized there were other kinds of art that were gone in an evening, a theater performance, for example. A play only exists as a script for a performance, a paper booklet, until actors take it up and make it live. Books can last forever.

"So the transitory nature of these murals," I said, still considering this, "is part of the whole process. Normally you're sculpting in marble where you're going for the ages, or you're painting in oils and carefully varnishing it as you think of it hanging in people's homes for five generations. But an intrinsic part of this project is that the murals are gone next week or next year. It's a totally different feel, isn't it?"

"Most of our murals are painted in three days' time. They're leaving their mark and when it's gone it's gone."

"Do you give tours of some of the murals?"

"I do, them every Monday Thursday, and Friday, at ten in the morning and two in the afternoon."

"There is enough interested traffic to do six tours a week?"

"Not all the time, and on some days there is zero. It can be too hot, or raining, or too cold. The expenses of the murals project are tremendous. We get no support from the government. The tourism department has nothing in their budget for us. Paint costs have gone way up. I've been working with Graffiti World since 2015. They do everything now and I'm mainly supporting it."

"What is Graffiti World?"

"After that first festival in 2013, visiting artists came through and I found walls for them. The Graffiti World guys took over the coordination of artists and murals in 2015. I met them on the street one day and we began to talk. They are three computer-geek type guys into graffiti. One is the artist with the network of the best artists from all over the world. I'm an old gringa, and this project needed to be in the hands of young Mexican creatives! We decided to do a project together and after another magical weekend, I said 'Guys, it's yours.' We've been working together since. They're terrific."

"Is there a concentration of artistic activity here in Guadalupe in other ways than just the murals?"

"We have a lot of artists here, but that's not any different from many other *colonias* in San Miguel.

Colonia San Antonio has its own art walk. Here we are called the arts district because of the murals."

"Do you think you could ever live in the States again?"

"No."

"That was quick. What have you learned by living in México that you couldn't have learned by staying in the States?"

"Acceptance."

"Of other ways of doing things?"

"More like acceptance of my own life's journey. I couldn't do this back in the States."

"Tell me about the mural we're going to look at today."

She pulled out an illustration. "This was done in 2016, although it looks like it could've been painted yesterday. It's by Sego, one of the most important artists in México. It's the favorite of everyone who comes through."

"What is it called?"

"*Achurado*. He was the leader of the Michoacán defense forces. He fought alongside his friends and neighbors, many of them lemon farmers. The painting style is line engraving, and it's a combination of acrylic and aerosol."

"All right. Let's go see it."

We climbed into Colleen's vintage SUV and

drove about a kilometer and a half through the irregular street grid of Guadalupe, passing many other murals. They mostly featured human or animal figures. At a building near a dry watercourse she pulled over. "Here is *Achurado*."

The image was a male figure, head and shoulders. It was about twice human height, painted against a dark background on a sectioned steel overhead door, the kind that can be raised to retract it. The right hand is elevated to bring a lemon to his mouth. He is wearing a feathered hat and a vest over a red-orange shirt. Over the left shoulder a viper's head approaches his ear, the body coiled around his neck. A locust perches atop the hat.

The skin, hair and beard are all rendered in curving parallel lines, as if you're looking at strands of colored yarn. Throughout the entire surface you can see the thousands of tiny cleats in the metal, standing up no more than a sixteenth of an inch, the kind often cast into steel flooring to keep it from being slippery underfoot. That texture plays against the image. It's like a highly realistic painting done on coarsely woven canvas. You are at once aware of the realism of the paint and the contradictory texture of the canvas fabric layer beneath it.

"This one is a keeper, it needs to last," I whispered to Colleen and we said goodbye.

CONCLUSION
DOES IT HELP TO MOVE TO MEXICO?

The answer depends on what and who you are trying to help. To the extent that this chapter's message is not included in Chapter One, then the answer must still be subjective, because we saw in that chapter that one idea of home is that it's simply where we have come to rest, in a most fundamental way. In that sense, México can easily be home, although not everyone will find it so who cannot tolerate a bit of edginess in their home's definition.

Sill, México is certainly adaptable. As I sit in my study, a dramatic room overlooking the Río Laja valley eastward into the mountains far away, at this moment a small flock of white egrets has flown past, scanning the valley lengthwise and headed north at my eye level, where they are about a hundred feet above the water. After all its transformations, the river is now about ten feet wide and you could cross it here without getting your knees wet. I work every day and I love to watch these wonderful birds pass, often more than once each way. Below, a small herd of multicolored goats is perusing the riverbank, intermittently visible under the cover of the trees. As I write this in late August, the time of year when the Río Laja still has some water, it is gradually drying up as the days grow shorter. As I have shown in earlier chapters, this changeable scene has come to frame my reality. This room is all glass on the valley side, and it sits directly on the white stone bluff. The drop from eight feet beyond my windows is equivalent to looking out from a ten-story building. If having the proper perspective is fundamental to a writer's vision, then this feels like the edge of the world.

Below me, a family of squirrels runs about unafraid of my presence above them. For hours they sit on the precise edge of the bluff. Are they sunning themselves? How do they get anything done? I know I work harder than they do.

This scene prompts me to embrace its longer view, a basic tool for every writer. Here, so far above the valley floor and thirty kilometers from the mountains to the east, that sense of perspective bears me up. It's a way of seeing many things at once from varying distances, an instant and comprehensive overview. If this valley were a fictional setting, it would be a way of watching what all my characters are doing at any given moment. Isn't this a feature we would like to have in our lives, whatever we're doing?

Clearly not every scene in México is as inviting as

this, although many await our discovery. It is a country of incredible beauty. I've traveled all over this nation working on my books, and still barely touched the surface. This setting is one of the reasons we bought this house. After writing many books on the second floor terrace of our former casa in town, covered but open on three sides, I was feeling the need of more weather protection, without losing the sense of working outside or nearly so. Here I have it both ways.

In Spanish, this is *un buen lugar*, literally a good spot, but in the larger sense as well of a benign place to come to earth. It supports what I want to do with my life, and support is a gift we all need to flourish. Here it is quiet, and although the valley weather has many faces, and a different dawn emerges out of the distant mountains each day, these moods mostly serve to remind me of my connectedness, because they cannot be ignored. My own biorhythms have been progressively reset and recalibrated to merge with and resonate to the ambience around me. I have said before that setting is always an important part of my fiction, always an actual character, and for that to be true, my perception of it must also be an important part of my focus. To answer a question I have asked others all through this book, yes it is home for us. It is where we work and live with a continual joy.

Our nearest neighbors, none of them human, are curious about us, as we are about them after our long sojourn in the city. Both the fox family (mom and dad and two kits), and the roadrunners have come up close to my windows and peered inside. The possum (here called the *tlacuache*) and her young have visited and were not much disturbed at what they observed. When they saw me return their gaze they did not run off. A five-foot long black king snake slithered past my windows not long ago. He is our rodent patrol, and I would never bother him. The same is true of the palm-sized tarantula we found last year outside our storeroom door. Skunks pass by in the night, sometimes too close. The terrain around us is interwoven with a network of paths of different sizes, all in active use. Last week driving in, I saw a rattlesnake crossing the lane not far from the end of our driveway. It was a trifle hair raising, but we are committed to get along with the critters that lived here before we arrived.

These mostly calm encounters have made me feel more at home here. The animal presence is more evident than that of the humans; there are only eight houses here on this sixty-acre stretch of bluff, and several of them are not continuously occupied. Because our property is nearly three acres, the road is almost a block away. In the busiest of times it carries about six or seven cars a day.

To return to our question, Does it help to move? Anyone reading this book as far as this point can see its effect on me. I also think anyone who reads this book is doing so because the question of living somewhere else is at least of some passing interest. I have tried to show that it is not a fairy tale or an idle dream. They are asking, I wonder what that would be like? Why would people do that? Can I see myself in that position, doing what some of these people do? If you were utterly content in your current situation you wouldn't have gone to that section on Amazon.com and come away with this book.

I never write even the first sentence of any book, fiction or nonfiction, without knowing who would wish to read it. Each book is personal, and they are never simply pitched out at random.

If you're retired and your lifestyle is inactive, moving may help only by providing a change of scene, something you can get easily enough of through travel within the United States or Canada. My impression of people who move to the interior of México is that they are actively in search of change, and active is the governing word. One major purpose of this book is to demonstrate how others have answered those same questions.

When we came to the San Miguel area I was retired from my business life, where I had started three small entrepreneurial companies. Two years before we left Minnesota I had become engaged in once again launching the writing career I had always wanted to have, but had never before been able to revive. Living in México not only provided me with a new terrain rich both in subjects and stimulation, but it also skewed my old perspectives and forced me to consider my life experiences in different ways, often merely to understand what I was looking at within myself. Stepping outside of our normal sphere can give us a genuinely fresh point of view, which is the essence of seeing things differently. More bluntly, it changed the filter through which I was used to viewing things and propelled me out of my rut. Nothing was lost other than a certain weary familiarity.

The essential point, though, is that I didn't move to México to slow down or kick back, and I didn't head first for the beach communities, although I do enjoy them now and then. Mainly I was seeking a change and a stimulus. I knew that my mind and my character were not finished growing. Nor was my 'creative arc,' that revealing term we heard from Alan Goldfarb.

So in respect of my own experience, the best way and possibly the only way to judge, I would have to answer, yes, it does help to move. The reorientation to all the new detail of life started my brain vibrating again, as it will yours. You are forced to answer questions you would never have thought to ask before. You are required to realize that people regard you in ways they never did at home. You are suddenly a minority, a foreigner, and you will be seen as more exotic that you have ever been before. You must be ready to field a series of challenges that you cannot anticipate. It will keep you limber, light on your feet, always a challenge later in life. Just for that reason (and the poor quality of the sidewalks), bring sensible shoes.

If you are open to change, even if you are seeking it within limits you define for yourself, then yes, you should consider such a move, just as you realize it's not for everyone. If serendipity is more interesting to you than certainty, then you may be a good candidate. I believe most of us are not wired to settle slowly into silence, to simply recede and stare without comment at the same scene passing us by every day. This place is not for those content to die in the house they grew up in. If you don't need to live life only on smooth pavement, everywhere and at all times, then México may be an option for you. As the poet Dylan Thomas wrote, "Do not go gentle into that good night." As far as I can tell, no one here is.

There is also an argument that you now know more than you ever did. For example, my writing career had an early start and then ran off the rails, and I was silent in that regard for more than thirty years. Having that career now in full flower, with a television deal pending for my mysteries in the last third of my life, is even better, because I know things today I could never have articulated, or perhaps even imagined, back then.

Despite the trumpeting of the press and the U.S. government, México is not a jungle (mostly, except for the Yucatán, with parts of Chiapas and Tabasco) full of vile snakes and hostile animals. It is more of a friendly place, full of cordial people with better manners than you have probably ever encountered before. To make your way here you need to realize that they will expect much the same politeness from you. It is a place where business is personal, where variety is an accepted and functioning part of everyday life. Here diversity is not a university course, a mere series of judgmental lectures, but always a commonplace reality. It is the way things work.

And while this town is no longer a good destination for people with no more than Social Security to get by on, the cost of living will still flatter your budget.

In an earlier chapter I wrote about specific things not to like about San Miguel and México in general, but however real, for me they do not change the bottom line: this is a fundamentally rewarding place to be.

So to finish a single line of enquiry, one of several that winds through this varied terrain, if you are open to the experience, it can easily become home, your home. As we have often heard as a cliché, home is where the heart is. While that is true, just as importantly or even more so, it's also where the mind and the soul are.

If this fits your profile and your goals, then yes, moving does help. It opens doors you had walked past many times because if you weren't looking for them, you didn't notice they were there. While many expats here are grandparents, they do not now live solely for their grandchildren. They also live for themselves because they understand that they are not yet finished with the very broad range of what living is and can be about. Nor are they are finished with pushing the boundaries back, and more than once. If you fit this description of how you would rather live, then that can be your path too. After all, each path is unique, and one of them belongs exclusively to you.

It beckons to you now, as it did to me and to many others who are my neighbors.

Exiles and immigrants are made, not born. We do not rise to deliver our valedictorian speech at high school graduation and begin with the words, "I just can't wait to get out of here!"

While we may still wish to get out from under the thumb of our parents, out into our own apartments or college dorms in a city larger than our small town in Ohio or Oklahoma, we tend to think of these changes as extensions of our previous life. Those changes still offer continuity, and they feel like the standard landmarks of growth and development. The decision to become an expat, an exile, or an immigrant comes later, and it is of a different order entirely.

The process of leaving one's homeland is one of growing divergence. It resembles a failing marriage, where each day we get up and discover ourselves slightly farther way from our partner. Eventually it becomes a fork in the road that as we approach it, can one day no longer be avoided. Taking either path is a commitment to avoid the other. Still, most people will choose the safer option to stay where they are, since the unknown is always more frightening than the familiar, no matter how ugly they know it to be, and will perhaps continue to be.

My final thought about home is this: what if the process for most expats has not been that we left home? Perhaps what happened, ever so gradually, was that home left us as it became progressively more distant from what we were, had been, and worse, more distant from what we wanted to become in the remainder of our lives, and was foreseeably going to end where we did not wish to follow.

All we did was to move on to a more welcoming place; one we hoped we would be happier to call home.

ONE LAST WORD

I have seen a number of books over the years that attempt to provide current residency and visa requirements for México. They are often out of date by the time they appear in print. Just in my eleven years here there have been several major revisions in the immigration process and requirements.

For shorter visits, the six-month tourist visa has

been constant. It is available at your border entry point if you drive in, or at the airport where you land. It can be renewed for another six months, an excellent trial period (reissued is a more accurate term), if you spend one night outside the country before coming back in. Long-term residency visas must be obtained at a Mexican consulate near where you live in the United States or Canada. The most up-to-date terms for obtaining these visas are best found online at a link the consulate can provide. Exact provisions may vary from consulate to consulate.

Knowing how to get in legally and comfortably is the most basic part of your homework. That's where your new life begins.